ESSEX
MURDER
CASEBOOK

STAN JARVIS

COUNTRYSIDE BOOKS

NEWBURY · BERKSHIRE

COUNTRYSIDE BOOKS
3 Catherine Road
Newbury, Berkshire

ISBN 185306 285 5

Designed by Mon Mohan

Produced through MRM Associates Ltd., Reading
Typeset by Paragon Typesetters, Queensferry
Printed by Woolnough Bookbinding, Irthlingborough

Contents

Acknowledgements

Historical research, in crime and punishment as in any other subject, requires work in national and local records of surprising diversity. My old friends and some new ones at the *Essex Chronicle* have been the main source of help with information and illustrations. The expert advice has come from my friend Inspector Maureen Scollan, author of *Sworn to Serve: Police in Essex* and Sergeant Fred Feather (retired), Curator of the Essex Police Museum. They made many useful suggestions and put all their records at my disposal.

A lot of basic reference work was done in the Chelmsford Library and the Essex Record Office. I thank all the staff who have helped me on a daily basis for their interest and help in obtaining recondite material.

I want to thank Nicholas and Suzanne Battle of Countryside Books and their helpful staff for seeing me through the birth of my sixth book produced by them.

There is one person who has supported and encouraged me through the writing of 20 books on Essex life and landscape, on Christian names and on the City of London – she is my wife Hazel. To her, with love and thanks, I dedicate this book.

Stan Jarvis
Summer 1994

1

IN THE THICK
OF THE ACTION

Essex had been subject to the laws of the Romans, Saxons, Danes and Normans as it became more closely and systematically inhabited in the first thousand years after the birth of Christ, and for the last millenium it has answered to English and British law. Records kept of crime and punishment cover only the last 500 years; from these we can see that murder has always been a relatively common crime, universally committed without qualification as to time, place or sex.

The difficulties of bringing a murderer to justice are demonstrated as far back as 350 years ago in the case of a victim, Thomas Kidderminster, a gentleman from Herefordshire who, in the course of personal business, put up at the White Horse Inn, Chelmsford in April 1654. Travel on horse was then fraught with danger during the disturbances of the Civil War, but Thomas had stayed at the White Horse on previous occasions and though he was carrying a large sum of money, he felt safe there.

From that night he was never again seen alive. His wife, expecting their baby, was anxiously awaiting his arrival in London where they were to meet. When he did not arrive she made allowances for the many ways in which a traveller could be delayed – bad roads, poor weather, complications of business – but when a couple of weeks had passed she did become fearful as to his safety and made all the enquiries she could. She did not know his exact route as he rode through Essex and no rumours reached her ears of men found dead or injured in the eastern counties. She became so desperate that when helpful people told her that they had seen a man of his description journeying to Holland on the one hand and 'Barbadoes' on the other she sent messages by merchants to inhabitants of those places begging for any possible sightings of her husband. When her baby was born and her own money had run out she had to take a job as a wet-nurse to keep herself and the baby, but she still sought news of her husband to the best of her limited ability.

Even eight years later, when she had been reduced to asking her sister in London to take her in she was still mourning the day he went away and puzzling over the total lack of news. One morning her sister, reading the sort of news pamphlet which preceded newspapers, cried out, 'Sister, here's news of your husband!' and read out: '... the bones of an unknown person, supposed to be robbed and murdered, were found buried in a back yard in Chelmsford ... ' The public was invited to give the coroner or the constable of Chelmsford details of anyone they knew to have been missing some time ago (the flesh had completely decomposed). Though her friends tried to persuade her to let the matter rest Mrs Kidderminster went to much trouble and expense to make further enquiries on this line and finally set out for Chelmsford on her own voyage of detection and investigation. She was at last successful. The murdered man was her husband, the murderers were the landlord of the White Horse and his wife, with their servants also implicated. But at the subsequent trial Mrs Kidderminster had no redress. The landlord had died years before, possibly poisoned by his wife, and she herself was dead before Mrs Kidderminster got to Chelmsford. The servants were put on trial, but the jury felt that the passage of time had made the recollections of witnesses too unreliable to enable a judgement to be made as to the measure of guilt of the surviving suspects.

Mrs Kidderminster's only consolation was that she now knew definitely of her husband's fate, that he was dead and she must now concentrate on what she was to do with the rest of her life.

There must have been many such cases of sudden disappearance all around the county in those wild and troubled days. Yet every village had its parish constable, organised as early as the 16th century, and he was responsible to an area constable who in turn served a chief constable for the county, reporting to the gentlemen of the county who became known as Justices of the Peace. They held their 'Sessions' or meetings every quarter when all the business of county administration was dealt with, from clearing ditches to trying witches, including the receiving of reports from parish constables as to the peace of their 'patches'. Trials of prisoners taken into custody for all kinds of offences were then held. All too often they included several cases of murder.

The system worked until the increase in population and the growth of villages into towns made closer supervision necessary, day and night, of a larger neighbourhood where crimes of all kinds were proliferating alarmingly. We have it from the pen of Henry Fielding (1707-1754), distinguished novelist and acknowledged originator of the present system of policing. His 'Inquiry' of 1750 reported an increase of robbery in London and laid out suggestions for tackling the problem. Official salaries paid to Fielding's picked men were very low, but they were a select band who became known as the Bow Street Runners, from the place of their headquarters. They made such an impact on London that crime there shrank abruptly, so the Government stopped paying for this new tiny 'police force'!

Reform of the criminal law and the creation of a proper police force in London had to wait until the appointment of Robert Peel as Home Secretary in 1820. By 1829 he had revised the sentences for all kinds of crime, removing the death penalty from more than a hundred offences. What is more, he suggested that central government should establish a proper police force for the London area, employing some 2,000 men for which he, as Home Secretary, would be ultimately responsible. This was the mould from which the local police forces covering Britain as a whole were eventually shaped.

In Essex the crime rate was soaring at this time because of the great hardship caused to agricultural labourers by the introduction of mechanised farm machinery at the onset of the Industrial Revolution. Men thrown suddenly out of work, and with no opportunities of other jobs in their rural situation, ganged together, broke the threshing machines, the reapers and binders which were ruining them, and in their anger burned their former employers' crops and the barns in which they and the machinery were kept. In 1829 a 16 year old labourer was publicly hanged on top of the great gate to Chelmsford prison for making his own individual protest at unemployment by burning down a barn on the farm where he had worked. In the following year a gang of 16 men who in hopelessness had damaged their farmer's new machinery, were torn from their families and mercilessly sent to penal servitude in the colony of Australia.

These desperate crimes brought the magistrates to a realisation of the terrible plight of rural working people. They met the Lord Lieutenant of Essex at the Shire Hall in Chelmsford and resolved to guard against the very real risk of open revolt in the county by drawing up lists of men who could be called upon to form a special force at a moment's notice. Thus was sown the seed of the Special Constabulary as we know it today. This did not cure the underlying cause of burgeoning crime – unemployment. By 1839 the atmosphere in Essex was very tense and a wholesale revolt was seen as a real possibility. It reflected the situation obtaining throughout the country, and the government was forced to listen to the representations made by county delegates about the conditions in Essex and the need for a much stronger, better organised county police force. On 24th July 1839 the County Police Bill was introduced into Parliament by the Home Secretary. Under this Act the Essex representatives asked the Secretary of State to approve their plan to appoint a chief constable and 115 superintendents and constables. The Essex County Police Force became one of the earliest and most efficient forces in the country, and it stays that way today.

Essex was extremely fortunate in that Captain John McHardy (RN), was appointed as its first Chief Constable and stayed at its helm for more than 40 years. He started his career in the Royal Navy in 1812, when he was ten, as a Boy Third Class, moving swiftly up the ladder of promotion through his gift for command and a display of personal bravery. By 1828 he had transferred to the Coast Guard as an inspecting commander where he came very much into contact with the criminal element in what was then a lucrative business – smuggling. His appointment dated from 11th February 1840, when there was much to be done in hammering out the best way forward in the organisation of this new police force, in the face of those die-hards who still insisted that this extra cost to the county was unnecessary. The majority of Essex people, however, were looking forward to this increased and county-wide organised police force complementing the old 'village constable' system. This continued while the county force developed its muscles to cope with the ever-escalating volume and variety of crime then being committed, especially in those rapidly developing areas contiguous to London. We shall see clear evidence of that situation in the case of the dreadful, vicious murder of PC Clarke in 1846.

Through 1840 the first three superintendents were interviewed and appointed by the new chief constable, and the first 15 policemen were being trained on the streets of Chelmsford. Not a large force, you might say, but initially the Act only allowed for it to be established 'experimentally' in addition to the existing system. Captain McHardy attended the meetings of the Justices of the Peace at the County Quarter Sessions when all the business of the county was done before prisoners were brought up for trial.

The first ever 'civilian' member of the Essex police force was Walter Burke who started work as secretary to McHardy on 1st March 1840. The Chief Constable was wise enough to know that the appointment of a uniformed superintendent to such a job could have caused envy and bitterness. Burke and his chief made do with a temporary office in Chelmsford Prison which had been built in 1828 up on Springfield Hill. By April they had moved to nearby Arbour Lane, taking over the military stores depot, despite protests from the Essex Militia. This was a strong sign of the importance now being attached by the government to the development of the new police force.

By the end of May 1840, the 100 policemen initially allowed by the Act had been recruited. McHardy could choose carefully; with the Essex agricultural labourer getting something like eight shillings a week, the policeman's pay of 19 shillings after training must have seemed like riches. There were strict conditions of employment. Many labourers of that day could not read or write and these were very necessary qualifications. It was found that an intermediate rank of men between superintendent and constable was necessary in the daily administration of the service, so 20 'inspectors' were appointed, either through promotion or by special recruitment.

Captain McHardy stayed as Chief Constable of Essex until 1881, when he was 80 years old! Such a situation could never be repeated, but it can be said that this man really set the county police force firmly on course for the continuing expansion, development and specialisations seen today. As the newly recruited force was trained at the police headquarters in what we now call 'Old Court' off Arbour Lane, they were seen in almost embarrassing numbers about the streets of Chelmsford. It was not long, however, before the county had been divided up into police districts with an inspector and his constables operating from their own local station. From there they would patrol to the boundaries of their area, to link up with neighbouring divisional patrols.

As well as their uniform they were provided with a 'rattle', a bit like the old bird-scarer, to sound the alarm, a lantern for night patrol and a baton or truncheon. Every policeman had to provide his own rucksack and notebook. Each division had its own transport – one horse and cart each. It took suspects in for questioning and on to Chelmsford gaol if necessary. It moved policemen, their families and their furniture to new postings and enabled inspectors and supervisors to get round the division and check their men at work. There was one snag: to avoid the extra cost of excise duty on more sophisticated carts they had to make do with an open one-horse, two-wheels only cart. But on the other hand by law it had to bear in white-painted letters the details of the owner: 'John Bunch Bonnemaison McHardy, Chief Constable, Chelmsford, Essex'. How that must have impressed the natives!

While the systems of the county and parish policing ran parallel there was bound to be some friction, but with the newspapers reporting faithfully the apprehension and trial of more criminals, those towns not yet won over to the new system were much impressed and gradually the traditional parish or village constables were replaced, adding to the prestige and efficiency of the burgeoning county force. Those towns which had formed their own local police forces under the 1835 Municipal Corporations Act, namely Colchester, Harwich, Maldon and Saffron Walden, could not afford a 24-hour policing programme, so they had to fall back on the old parish constable system still in operation for those difficult days and nights when coverage was sketchy. The county police service became more attractive as it put into operation its plans for building new stations and obtaining modern equipment.

By 1850 the new police were well in their stride, encouraging a more professional attitude towards the systematic investigation of murder and other serious crimes. In the accounts of murder recounted in these pages there can be traced the continuous development and sophistication of police methods which were to lead to the amazing techniques and equipment used in the employment of blood groups, DNA testing, helicopters and heat-seeking observation which our county police now employ. The police showed great devotion to duty in this new concept of policing, and as they achieved greater success in detection and conviction they were the target of desperate criminals who would kill mercilessly rather than be caught. Policemen like George Clarke, only 20 years old, paid the supreme price in the performance of their duty. This price has been paid by many more policemen down to our time. The particularly cruel murder of PC Gutteridge in 1927 is a typical example. Sad to say, that ultimate risk in every policeman's life continues into our own times, in Essex as elsewhere. Detective work in the early days was part of the ordinary policeman's daily workload. Inspector Maureen Scollan, in her excellent work, *Sworn to Serve: Police in Essex 1840-1990* gives a good example: 'Captain McHardy expected his policemen to be able to use their initiative when necessary, and in November 1851 the *Essex Standard* reported a smart piece of detective work at Great Coggeshall where initiative had been used. Having failed to arrest a man they wanted, Constables Smith and Oakley dressed as distressed labourers, and went from door to door selling matches. As their suspect opened his door to buy the matches, he was arrested.'

When the Captain answered questions on his Essex force before a House of Commons select committee in May 1853 he stated that his force then numbered 202 men, and its successful introduction had encouraged neighbouring counties to follow suit. His next improvement was the introduction of the rank of sergeant, between inspector and constable, paying two shillings and sixpence a week more than the constable's wage. The service flourished. In 1857 a government inspector reported that it was one of the most efficient in the country – a pattern that other forces followed with

Left, an Essex policeman posing in front of Chelmsford railway viaduct and right, Constable, and later Sergeant, 'Zepp' Smith who apprehended the crew of a downed Zeppelin in 1916. *(Essex Police Museum)*.

confidence, while the old town services were struggling to maintain even a rudimentary service. A year later Harwich and Saffron Walden decided to merge with the county which, by 1870, had 20 police stations mustering 53 cells between them, as well as a large number of police houses.

The introduction of railway travel from about 1845 helped to move numbers of policemen quickly when the situation required, but those divisional carts were still literally the 'workhorses' of the county force. People generally were now much more mobile through the facility of the train service and the excursions organised to places like Southend. At the same time it gave criminals opportunities to extend their areas of operation. The duties of the policeman were also extending into fresh fields. Let three examples demonstrate the variety; the inspection of food under the Food and Drugs Acts, the checking of the compulsory vaccination of children, and even the checking of the proper insulation of telegraph wires.

The great milestone on the force's way to modern times was the retirement of McHardy (now promoted by the Navy to Admiral) as

Chief Constable on 31st October 1881. He enjoyed little more than a year in retirement, dying in December 1882. His successor, Major William Poyntz, soon started issuing orders, beginning with a smartening up of his policemen's appearance – even their staves, equivalent to today's truncheons, had to be cleaned and varnished regularly. By this time Essex was suffering from its closeness to London and its notorious East End. Criminals would fan out from the metropolis by train or trap or Shanks's pony, commit their thefts, their assaults, and then catch a train back to safety and anonymity in the great city. Such a man murdered Inspector Thomas Simmons on the Romford Road in January 1885. In this case the murderer was arrested at a Euston pawnbroker's when he tried to pawn the gun he had used. It was Major Poyntz who encouraged his men to read and take an interest in wider cultural activities. Under his command a police force library was instituted which continued long after he retired in July 1888.

His death coincided almost exactly with the introduction of a new unit in local government – the County Council. Maureen Scollan puts it in a nutshell: 'Instead of being responsible to a body of justices from influential families, police became accountable to a powerful standing joint committee of elected county councillors and non-elected justices.' It was Captain Edward Showers who had to see the police service through the change-over from 1st April 1889. The provisions of the Act concerning the local police forces still operating obliged the five man Maldon force to surrender its powers to the county force, which then totalled 315 men, while their head constable became a county force inspector. So, only Colchester continued as an independent force. There was also a new force formed of just four men, to act as river police in the protection of the oyster-laying on the Colne estuary. They had a boat bought for them, as well as two dinghies. People may have smiled, but the local oystermen thought the world of them!

The usefulness of the county force was clearly illustrated in that same year of the change-over when it was asked to send a large force to Tilbury Docks where a particularly violent strike was in progress. The policemen of the day may have had some sympathy with the strikers in their fight for better pay, but the security of their jobs and the valuable 'perks' of pensions and gratuities still kept the police slightly apart from their fellow working men. They also had the rather doubtful advantage of compensation for their dependants if they were killed on duty. Elizabeth Eves was the recipient of such compensation after her husband Acting Sergeant Adam Eves was brutally beaten to death when challenging four men who had stolen sacks of grain from Hazeleigh Hall Farm. The full story is told in *Essex*

Headlines. The telephone is taken totally for granted today; a hundred years ago it was a minor miracle when this strange instrument used the thinnest of wires to connect police voices and ears between Chelmsford, Brentwood and Romford. Such a useful means of quick distribution of police information was rapidly expanded countywide. The new County Police Headquarters, opened at Chelmsford in 1903, is now but a nucleus of additions in various architectural styles as expansion and development of the service has advanced.

One important development, long since outmoded, was the provision of a bicycle, for in rural areas the village bobby faced beats of up to 20 miles in a shift. Before they were official equipment one old friend of mine, long since deceased, could remember using his own bicycle, but hiding it in the hedge before the inspector made a rendezvous with him on the beat, using the divisional horse and cart. It was a horrible night of rain and wind. Though the inspector knew about the bike he told the bobby it was such a terrible night that he should go back to base with him in the cart. He knew the poor fellow would have a long walk back at the end of the shift to pick up that bike! My friend was mightily pleased when the new rule came in.

Though the motor carriage was being produced in numbers as the police service continued into the present century the force itself did not own a single car, even though many a motorist was flagrantly exceeding the speed limit of twelve miles per hour, as the Chief Constable told the County Council meeting in October 1900. Two police officers had to take their bicycles and use stop watches either end of a measured stretch of road to provide a reliable test of speed, and even then a good barrister could punch holes in their evidence. At that time cars were still the status symbol of the influential county people in the upper income bracket, which put the police in a difficult position.

Captain Showers plugged away in committee meetings on the advantages of a car to his force – even just one car – but he was not successful until 1909 when he was allowed to rent, annually, just one car, and that arrangement continued down to 1916, by which time it was a very much more common form of transport, and the Chief Constable was at last allowed to buy – just one. The bobby on his beat, riding his bike, and metaphorically keeping his ear to the ground around his particular 'patch' was still worth 20 cars or more. We shall see how local gossip, faithfully reported and carefully sifted, started an enquiry at Moat Farm, Clavering, which finally brought murderer Samuel Dougal to book.

Difficulties like the secession of Southend from the county police to set up its own service as a newly created County Borough were overtaken by the far more important national involvement in the First World War from 1914. Some most unexpected responsibilities devolved upon the police, who lost large numbers of experienced officers in the rush to the colours. Maureen Scollan points out that in the first year of war only 59 of the 468 sergeants and policemen could be granted their annual leave in order that a minimum level of policing be maintained. Captain Showers gave up the unequal struggle and resigned along with his deputy, Raglan Somerset. Showers moved on to the more homely position of Acting Chief Constable of the Colchester 'outfit' for the rest of the war. The new man, Captain John Unett, was able to introduce some of his ideas with the necessities of war acting in his favour, especially in his overhaul and expansion of the organisation of the Special Constabulary.

Post-war strikes by the police affected the Metropolitan and Liverpool areas but left Essex untouched. Its men benefited from the negotiations leading to the Police Act of 1919 which at last made conditions of work and rates of pay applicable throughout the country, though the severe economic difficulties of the time could not allow some of the improvements and developments nationally agreed. During the General Strike of 1926 the Essex police stayed

Motorcycle police checking a motorist's speed with a radar gun at South Woodham Ferrers in January 1990. *(Essex Chronicle)*

loyal to their oath of service. It was less than a year later that an individual policeman, loyal to his oath, performed the simple duty of stopping what he suspected was a stolen car, only to be shot dead in the road. He was PC Gutteridge. His story is recounted in the following pages.

Car and motorcycle patrols were introduced in 1930, operating by day and night, but the stringent demands of government economy denied any real expansion. Chief Constables came and went, but their hands were tied until, with Captain Peel's appointment in 1932, there began an increase in establishment and accordingly in equipment, cars and so on. Yet the first public broadcast message by Essex police had to wait until 1942. There had been a fatal accident on the Stone Bridge at the bottom of Chelmsford's High Street, but no witnesses had come forward, so a police car toured the town clearly and loudly asking anybody who had seen anything relevant to the accident to come forward. Sad to say, this inspired innovation was fruitless. Two-way radio conversation between cars and HQ was not introduced until the late 'forties.

The patient research required of the CID was demonstrated at this time in the investigation of the murder of nine year old Pamela Coventry at Hornchurch in January 1939. This case, as we shall see, also showed the frustration the police must often experience when the evidence gathered so painstakingly does not lead to a conviction. The Criminal Investigation Department was introduced at Scotland Yard in 1842 as an elite force of just six detectives. By 1921, as George Totterdell of the Essex County Police tells us in *Country Copper* (1956) '...a notice appeared in orders that applications would be considered for admission to the Criminal Investigation Department of the Essex County Force. I immediately put my name down, and on April 1 1921 I was appointed to the CID', But in Essex there had been three sergeants and ten constables employed on detective duty, in plain clothes, as early as 1888.

Passing over the alarums and excursions of the Second World War we see the Essex Police Force emerging with just two fatalities and looking forward to modernisation and to full manning, or staffing, to be politically correct, for the Women's Auxiliary Police Corps had been formed in 1941. The separate Colchester constabulary was at last taken into the county force in 1947, with obvious advantages for service to the public. A year later two-way police car radio connection to a transmitting station was set up when 26 cars were equipped. Further developments at national level led to the integration into the county service of the last of the separate police forces, that of the County Borough of Southend. The amalgamation was bitterly resisted but resolutely pushed through, to take

Essex policewomen being trained by Inspector Johnson, April 1977. *Essex Chronicle*

effect from 1st April 1969. Now the police force was truly Essex. In this context we must not forget the section started in 1948 to patrol the Thames in tandem with the Kent constabulary, and the river police, as the public know them, extended its coverage to other estuaries, based on Southend, Bradwell and Burnham, as well as at Tilbury.

There have been many changes and 'tidying-up' of the county police force since then. For example, the Romford police division was transferred to the Metropolitan Police in 1965. The development of technological 'warfare' against crime since then has been almost too complicated to be thoroughly understood by the general public, from helicopters with heat-seeking cameras to computerised 'photofits' and DNA tests for positive identification.

The public in Essex is appreciative of its police force. It cannot guarantee us freedom from criminals, from accidents, from natural disasters, but its watchfulness does discourage thousands of would-be criminals, its patient investigations do bring hundreds of offenders to justice, and the appearance of policemen on our streets and at our public events is so relaxed, yet so reassuring, that the old advice, 'ask a policeman' is still followed today. But let murderers beware, the Essex police force has very long arms.

2

THE LEANING TOMBSTONE

THE MURDER OF HENRY TRIGG AT BERDEN,
MARCH 1814

The tombstone does not actually give much information. It can hardly be read today – just a name 'Henry Trigg' and the date '25th March 1814'. It is crooked with age, worn by wind and weather, but nevertheless worthy of our respect for it reminds us of the death of a brave man. It stands in the churchyard of the village of Berden in the far north-west of Essex. In the parish register of burials we can read: '1814. March 25th. Henry Trigg, aged 36 years. The Street, Berden.' An asterisk refers us to the bottom of the page, where a note has been added, dated 1899, 'On the tombstone . . . it is stated that he was murdered on 25 March 1814, the burial would doubtless be a few days afterward'. Henry was a shoemaker with a small shop on the village street right next to the entrance to the yard of Berden Hall, a fine old mansion in the Tudor style, but built in 1650.

The peace of this remote, quiet and pretty village was shattered one night by the sound of shooting and shouting. Next morning the dreadful news was buzzing round Berden like a swarm of bees; there had been a burglary at the shoemaker's on the Street and poor Henry Trigg was dead. He had been such a worthy man, unmarried, sharing his house with his parents, and his shoemaking with his father. More than that he had willingly shouldered the burden when it came to his turn to serve as village constable in those days when each community was as responsible for the prevention of crime as it was for the care of its own poor or the repair of the parish church. The only weapon he carried, handed down to each constable, was a stout staff.

It was not likely that crime and violence crossed his mind as the early spring sun set in the dusk of 25th March 1814. There had

17

been rumours of a gang of robbers roaming over the district on both sides of the county's border with Hertfordshire, but there was little to attract them to this small village. Henry made the place as secure as he could as a matter of habit and soon had the shutters up. His parents were in their late sixties – a good old age for those times. They had become more and more dependent on him for their daily bread and their security so Henry wanted them to feel safe at night. He slept in the room at the back of the shop and they had the upstairs room.

That very night thieves did break in. One of them, Thomas Turner, had already 'cased' the shop a fortnight before, in the process of going to the village to buy a dog from a man named Chapman. Turner's mate, William Pratt, the moving spirit in their criminal outings, told him to look round while he was passing through Berden to see if there was anything to make a midnight visit worthwhile. Turner reported that he did see something very interesting; bundles of leather, all prepared for shoemaking and ranged on shelves in Henry Trigg's shop, and the locks did not look too difficult. It all seemed very convenient to a couple of crafty housebreakers.

It was approaching midnight and the last candle in this truly sleepy village had been snuffed; the night was dark. Everything favoured the thieves. They did not know that Henry was there, right behind the shop. He heard their first fumbling at the door and guessed what was afoot. His first thought was for his parents. He crept up to their bedroom, woke them and told his father he was going down again to confront the intruders, but he might be glad of his help. By the time the old chap could come to his senses and get down the stairs Henry was already tackling Turner and Pratt with great courage and determination. He had used his constable's staff to good effect, and having knocked Turner down he was grappling with him on the floor. When he shouted to his father to give him a hand, Mr Trigg threw himself down across the fellow's legs and told his son to sit down hard on their captive.

The taller man, Pratt, now took command of the situation. It was impossible to separate friend from foe in the inky blackness so he fired a shot from a pistol over the heads of the three struggling men. It startled them so much that they all jumped to their feet. They could just see Pratt outlined against the night at the open door as he shouted at Henry Trigg, 'You damned rascal, I'll do for you!' He raised another pistol and fired again. The bullet hit Henry Trigg on the left upper side of his body, passed through his lungs and lodged in his spine. His loving mother, hovering anxiously at the door to the stairs saw her son 'drop like a bird' as she said afterwards. His father,

'Now, Damn your heart, I'll do for you!' *(Essex Police Museum)*

shocked and stunned, stood staring in disbelief while the burglars ran off for all they were worth, panting with exertion and relief at their lucky escape. They had no booty. Twenty pounds of leather which they had bundled into two sacks was flung aside and they left behind a 'dark lanthorn' and a hat. Henry Trigg died on the spot. Despite the efforts of neighbouring village constables no trace could be found of the direction in which the murderers ran. The dark night had ruled out any possibility of identification. Henry's parents said they could only tell their son apart from the thieves because his white shirt gleamed in that darkness.

A newspaper reporter sent out to cover the crime wrote: 'The loss of this young man to his father and mother is particularly affecting. With an unblemished character for honesty, sobriety, and civility, Mr Trigg had, by his industry, for some time past, cheerfully performed the duty of providing for his aged parents.' The shouting and the shooting and the wailing of despair brought people from their beds, including Mr Isaac Hodges from neighbouring Berden Hall. By 1st April members of the London police force, very interested in the growing number of crimes in this area of Essex and Hertfordshire, had attended at the scene of the crime, in the persons of Bow Street officers Vickery and Bishop. After several days of investigation and enquiry of the natives they left without finding a clue to the identity of the malefactors. The thieves must have congratulated themselves on their lucky escape with just a few bruises from that constable's staff. They laid low for a while, and the villagers buried their constable in sorrow, then took up again the necessary work and worry of their daily life.

Autumn came and went, winter was well on the way when, in January 1815, the Bow Street Runners received some information about other crimes which had been committed on the Essex/Hertfordshire border very close to Berden. It was a strong enough lead to send the Chief Clerk of the Runners down to Bishops Stortford with a posse of his men. They searched the houses of two men identified in the process of several robberies. One of these men was William Pratt, and how rewarding the tip-off proved. In his wretched little house in the town they found a large collection of keys made to pick all kinds of locks, several pistols made ready for firing and one of those shaded lanterns which could be instantly darkened to a pinpoint of light. They took Pratt into custody immediately. Either the Runners had further information, or Pratt squealed on his partner, for the police went straight to Thomas Turner's house nearby.

Having secured their prisoners and lodged them in Hertford gaol they tried on them the hat that witnesses had said was left behind in the shop where Henry Trigg was murdered. It fitted perfectly on Thomas Turner's head, but he knew what flimsy evidence that would be, saying, 'I wonder how many other men's heads in Stortford this hat will fit!' This was the only possible though diaphanous clue to their possible implication in the Berden attack, but through the suspicions engendered by the searches of their houses the two men were closely confined in Hertford gaol, isolated in separate cells, and left to stew for a while.

A confession was not long in coming from these frightened petty criminals who never intended murder as an outcome of their burglary expeditions. It was Turner who broke first. He sent a message to the chief gaoler that he wished to speak to him in private. He was taken from his cell to the added privacy of the gaoler's house. There he unburdened himself of all the panic and horror of that dark night in the shoemaker's shop. He insisted that it was not his hand which aimed the pistol and fired the fatal shot. Gaoler Wilson was very efficient; he took Turner's confession down in writing, returned Turner to his cell and sent for Pratt. To him he read his partner-in-crime's confession, and from him heard, after some hesitation, that what Turner had said was quite true, except that it was Turner who shot Henry Trigg. Of course, this was not likely as Trigg's father could witness that, despite the darkness, he could tell it was Turner who was struggling with him and his son when the first shot was fired. Pratt's confession was then committed to paper. Now they could both be taken before magistrates in Hertford where, again, they made 'a voluntary and ample confession of their guilt, but each criminated the other with actually having fired the pistol which killed the deceased' as the newspaper reported on 15th March 1815.

Although they had been concerned in other crimes in Hertfordshire, the murder of Henry Trigg at Berden was their most serious offence and so they were transferred to the gaol in Chelmsford to await trial at the Essex Assizes due to be held in a few days time. Here the confessions were read out again, supported by the testimony of the examining magistrates from Hertford while the Bow Street Runners Vickery and Bishop gave an account of their investigations, and then the judge, Mr Justice Chambre summed up the facts of the case for the jury. He prefaced his remarks with the observation that there had been far too many offences of this kind presented at this Assize. He charged the jury that if each of the prisoners had been present and were openly supporting each other in the murder committed in the course of the attempted burglary then they were equally guilty of that murder. If the jury could not believe the evidence as it had been presented then both men should be acquitted. The jury needed no time to dwell on it, they immediately declared both men guilty of murder. Observers said that neither man seemed much affected, outwardly, on hearing the sentence of death pronounced. Their end was swiftly arranged. On Monday 13th March 1815, quite early in the morning the guilty men were brought from the Chelmsford prison, then down by the river, near the old stone bridge built in 1787, and placed on the platform of the gallows overlooked by that bridge. The news of the execution had got round the town and a much larger crowd than usual for such a grisly spectacle had long since taken up the best viewing points. Pratt and Turner left this world in silence. It was obvious that in the many other crimes they had committed accomplices would have been involved, but the honour among thieves was observed.

Their bodies were later collected from the prison by a group of local surgeons, to be used for the good of humanity in medical training and research. Local criminals were warned by the rather righteous Chelmsford paper: 'May they take warning and depart from such wicked practices ere the same fate overtakes them, and they suffer the like ignominious end.'

3

A CASE OF GUILTY CONSCIENCE

THE MURDER OF DANIEL HOLT AT LEXDEN,
JANUARY 1788

How long could you lead a normal life with the fear of discovery that you were a murderer hanging over you? One man coped with such a burden, never expressing a word of regret or repentance for nearly 35 years before he blurted out his confession. But let us begin at the beginning.

Daniel Holt was 55 years old when he went to work his watermill at Lexden near Colchester on a cold winter's day in the first week of January 1788. A miller who ground the corn the villagers had grown was a well-known figure in the small community of the 18th century village. He was not always well-liked because some of those hard-working village labourers thought that he took more than his fair share of the flour their crop produced. Daniel worked a long day when the river's flow was full enough to set his machinery whirling. When he did not come home for his supper that night the family was not unduly worried, he might work on by lantern light if he had a lot of grain. On the other hand, he was a man who liked a drink and a yarn with friends in taverns as far away as Colchester.

But when he did not turn up that night or through the next day family and friends did become alarmed. They looked high and low for him, through Colchester and beyond they sent the message of his strange disappearance. Not a trace of him was found – and for 14 days or so the family was left in doubt and despair. While they waited fearfully a fisherman in East Donyland, some six miles downstream of Daniel's mill, was about to cast his line into the river Colne when he saw a strange object moving sluggishly in the ripples of the water. To his horror he realised it was a human body, much damaged by its exposure over a long period in the water and by some wounds which it may have sustained while alive.

The angler went crying for help and a party of men gathered to pull the corpse out on to the river bank. Someone then recognised the likeness and the garb as that of Daniel Holt. Another remembered the hue-and-cry raised by the village constable when he went missing. They thought at first that he must have committed suicide by throwing himself in his own mill pond.

Daniel's family were told of his fate and a coroner's inquest was convened to 'sit on the body' as it was quaintly put in the language of the day. They viewed the corpse and saw there were injuries to the head which could not have been caused by a fall or any collision with a hard object as the body drifted downstream, but they could not come to any resolution on the mystery, so they declared that death was accidental. Daniel was buried in Lexden churchyard and a note was duly made in the parish register of burials: '1788 January 20. Daniel Holt, aged 55.' The clerk did not think to record the unusual circumstances of his death.

From that day on for no less than 35 years no more was heard of this 'accidental' death, then once again it became a matter of gossip and speculation in the village beerhouses for miles around, spreading through Colchester market and on into the hinterland, and all because two men fell out. William Lester and Charles Williams lived within half a mile of each other in Colchester. They had known one another for 20 years or more and had never quarrelled. In fact they had often traded personal details over a glass of porter in the Fleece Tap in the town. One night Lester was sitting there, minding his own business, when in walked Williams around seven o'clock. Perhaps he had been drinking elsewhere, for he was in a very confiding mood. He sat straight down by Lester and, between sips from his mug, asked him if he had ever heard of old Daniel Holt who died all those years ago. Lester said he did not know the old chap or anything about him.

Williams obviously wanted to impress him. 'I know he was murdered,' he said, 'I was there, I helped another man to do it. He was hit over the head with a crow-bar.' He went on to tell the whole story. Daniel Holt had been in the Blue Pig at Colchester enjoying one glass too many. He staggered out of the tavern but only got to the steps leading up to the house next door when he slumped down and fell into a drunken sleep. Williams and his mate Roger Mundsey were still about even as late as midnight on this cold January night. Perhaps, like Daniel Holt, they were well insulated with alcohol. Nobody will ever know why these two foolish fellows took it into their heads to interrupt the miller's drunken doze, or what possessed Mundsey to pick up a crow-bar and strike Daniel brutally over the head.

The foolhardiness of this piece of mischief, and the gout of blood which gushed down the man's coat and out on to the doorstep must have cleared their drunken minds. They got an old sack from the yard behind the Blue Pig, stuffed the lifeless body in it and hauled it into the cellar of that tavern through a door which gave on to the street. Then they purloined a sack of sawdust from the same place to soak up as much of the blood as they could before trying to wash the rest of it off.

This was the end of Williams's confession apparently, so Lester could not, later, elaborate on the eventual disposal of the body into the river Colne, though he could say that the Blue Pig was about a mile from it. Lester was appalled that a man could so casually talk of the taking of a human life, but he had sworn himself to secrecy, so he could do nothing about it. For about three or four weeks he kept that secret, but his wife noticed that he was becoming a changed man. He could not sleep at night, he became so withdrawn and preoccupied that his wife was being made to suffer for Daniel Holt's murder. His health, too, deteriorated and he became so miserable that, in the end he blurted it all out to his wife. Either Williams told other people when he was in his cups in the weeks that followed, or Lester's wife just could not hold to her promise and sought comfort from her friends, for, three years from that night of confession, the gossip grew to such an extent in Colchester and in Lexden that the parish officers felt they must take some action to clear the matter up once and for all. After Williams brought Lester before a magistrate for slander the officers interviewed Lester and arranged for a case to be made to submit to 'the solemn enquiry of a court of justice'. And so it came to the Essex Spring Assizes in March 1823.

Williams had been arrested and was delivered from the gaol that morning to stand in the dock. Before the case was tried, however, the Lord Chief Baron, Sir Richard Richards spoke generally to the Grand Jury about the cases coming before them: ' . . . In one of these cases – a charge of murder – it is one of the most serious in my memory . . . you are to inquire whether murder was committed or not. Now, it may be difficult, at such a distance in time, to afford evidence of a murder being committed; but you will learn that the body was taken out of a river, where it is not impossible that the man might have accidentally fallen in . . . You will find that there is no evidence of any suspicions whatsoever having fallen upon the prisoner, excepting that about three years past the prisoner, when at an alehouse, confessed that he had murdered the man 35 years ago. Certainly some men have been fools enough to admit themselves guilty of crimes of which they were perfectly innocent. If the confession is proved, it will have its just weight upon your minds, whether or not at the time he made the confession he spoke the truth, as he might, or might not. The man to whom he made the confession appears never to have spoken of it until the present occasion. Upon such evidence you will determine whether you can possibly find a bill for murder, or even for manslaughter.'

This extraordinary trial for murder, noised around the county town of Chelmsford, stirred tremendous interest and the court was packed when it came on in March 1823. The charge against Charles Williams, then aged about 53, was that he wilfully murdered Daniel Holt of Colchester in 1788, by striking him on the head with an iron crow-bar. The prosecution made the point that, when the body was recovered from the river it showed marks of injury about the head which gave rise to the publicly expressed opinion at that time that Mr Holt had died a violent death. That was the belief in the neighbourhood, despite the coroner's jury concluding that the death was accidental. 'The probabilities of the case strongly supported that opinion, for, had the deed been a suicide, the marks of violence on the head would be unaccountable. The presumption therefore was that he had been first murdered and then thrown into the river.'

The local paper, the *Chelmsford Chronicle*, the only one for the county at that time, went into a purple passage over it:

'After a lapse of 35 years, which must have swept away half the race of mankind then living, it was not likely that there would be many witnesses now alive to give any account of the transaction. A coroner's inquest had been summoned on the body, surgeons were examined, and other persons had seen the remains of the deceased; but of all those but one individual survived. The coroner, the jury, the surgeons, all were dead, except one person who, through the inscrutable wisdom of Providence, had been spared to give evidence, upon a transaction so mysterious and important. This witness would prove the probable fact that Mr Holt had been deprived of life by violent means. He saw the body after it had been taken from the water – was present when it was examined by surgeons and he would distinctly state that the head had such injuries visible upon it as plainly indicated the mode in which the unfortunate man had been bereft. This fact was most important, as far as it went, to confirm the evidence by which the horrible crime of murder was charged upon the prisoner at the bar.'

The paper goes on to point out that Charles Williams was in court now through his own voluntary confession to a friend, that he was present at the attack, and aided and abetted another man in the vicious use of that iron crow-bar on Daniel Holt's head. 'The supposed confession was voluntarily made by the prisoner, at a public house at Colchester, to a man named Lester, so long as three years. The parties were sober, and in a state of mind as to remove all doubt as the consciousness of each upon the gravity of the conversation.' It then paraphrases part of the judge's address to the jury, saying that it must be very cautious in this situation even though, in general, a confession was the most conclusive and satisfactory evidence of guilt, and in a case like this, saved the trouble of a long and troublesome investigation as to the manner of the death and the motive for its perpetration.

Now the stage was set, a rustle of expectation spread round the court as people craned forward to see this one witness and hear his words. Esau Ladbrook stepped up: 'I am 64 years of age. I knew Mr Daniel Holt when he lived at Lexden. I saw his body when he was dead: I saw it in an outhouse near the River Colne, from whence it had been taken. I observed, when the doctor had taken off the skin, two bloody specks on the skull bone, on the left-hand side.' On cross-examination he added, 'This was 35 years ago. I saw the body at Donyland; this place was three miles from the Blue Pig. If the body had been thrown into the river at Colchester it might have floated up to Donyland if the tide set that way. The face of Mr Holt had not been disfigured by the crabs, or things of that sort. The doctors said there were no fractures on the head – there wasn't a fracture – I know. I saw no appearance of a cut or a stab upon any other part of his body.'

Just as Ladbrook was the only witness to the finding of the body, so William Lester was the only witness to the confession. He said how he had told his wife of it about a month later and 'about two or three years later' he shared his awful secret with Mr Hill, the landlord of the Fleece. He said that he had met Charles Williams several times since he made that confession and that he, Williams, had not shown any inclination to run away, even when the local gossip became so strong. But Williams did tell Lester that his revelation of that guilty secret had put his life in danger. It seems that the two men had fallen out over Lester's betrayal, for Williams had later brought Lester before a magistrate to charge him with slander and that was where the full story was told which set this trial in motion.

A couple of other witnesses added little further information. Elizabeth Buckingham, daughter of the landlord of the Blue Pig, was still alive; she remembered Daniel Holt being in the house that night, in the parlour with 'two bad women'. The grating to the cellar was in that very room, sometimes it was even left open, yet she never heard of a dead body, blood or sawdust ever being there. John Belander, son-in-law of the Blue Pig's landlord averred that on the night Daniel Holt died the cellar door fronting the street was firmly shut and locked.

The judge's decision was final: 'From the nature of the case, as proved by the witnesses, it would be impossible to convict the prisoner of the present charge'. He therefore directed the jury to bring in a verdict of not guilty. No one now will ever know the truth of Daniel Holt's death.

4

A POLICEMAN DIES

THE MURDER OF PC GEORGE CLARKE AT DAGENHAM,
JULY 1846

In July 1846 it was a murder so sensational that a week later crowds of people were still trailing into a cornfield near Dagenham, then a village, to see the flattened corn where one man had made his last struggle for life. They streamed out from places as far afield as Romford, Ilford and Barking, Chigwell and Hornchurch. There was nothing for them to see – the field, and those around it where corn and potatoes were well into growth, had already been trampled down by the police in their meticulous search for clues.

First they came upon a policeman's staff, at the same time they were assailed by an awful smell. The staff was lying in a ditch between fields of corn and potatoes. It was much battered and cut, looking as if it had been used in defence against a sharp axe-like weapon. The smell of death and decomposition told the searchers that a body must be lying nearby. A little further on they saw a policeman's cutlass caught up in the hedge between the fields. Looking inwards from that hedge was the object of their quest, the body of PC Clarke, so terribly injured and so viciously mutilated that without his uniform he could not have been recognised. The back of the poor man's head had been totally beaten in and, as a last savage indignity, he had been scalped, and that scalp had been laid down by his side. The policemen who found the body were profoundly affected by the gruesome and horrible sight.

A surgeon was sent for to note at the scene of the crime all the wounds inflicted. Then, when they took up the body to carry it away, they found that the policeman in his dying moments had been flung down so hard that his body had made an indentation in the field. More than one policeman was overcome by the sight of this cruelly mutilated body as they carried it to the comparative shelter of a ruined old house near what was then known as the Three Wantz, a little north of the village where three roads met.

1840

The uniform PC Clarke would have worn when he set out for his last patrol from Dagenham in 1846.

Elliott O'Donnell captures the atmosphere of the area at that time: 'In the 'forties of the last century few places around London held a more unenviable reputation than Dagenham in Essex; and for this reason: the flat, marshy ground between Dagenham and the Thames was haunted by gangs of smugglers, thieves, poachers, and desperate ruffians of all kinds, who hid in hovels and old hulks in the daytime and wandered abroad at night, rendering the fields and towns bordering on the Thames utterly unsafe for respectable citizens. Cries of murder proceeding from the waterside were of frequent occurrence after dusk, and those who heard them shivered and hastened on.'

The *Chelmsford Chronicle* disclosed the name of the unfortunate policeman in its issue of 10th July 1846: 'It is our painful duty this week to record the commission of one of the most barbarous murders that has ever disgraced the annals of this county. The victim was a steady, well conducted young man, named George Clarke, a metropolitan police-constable of the K division, from Dagenham.' The sorry story, as related at the subsequent inquest, begins on Monday 29th June 1846 at 9 pm, when four constables were marched out by the sergeant, as was then the custom, to take up the start of their beats for the night. The first man to be dropped off, 20 minutes later, was K313 Constable George Clarke. He was to cover his beat and meet his opposite number PC Kimpton, K340, at one o'clock in the morning at the crossroads called, in the old Essex dialect, the Four Wantz, where the roads ran to Dagenham, Ilford, Hornchurch and Chigwell. Apparently Clarke did not turn up, and Kimpton could not wait about because he had his own strict timetable to adhere to.

But Sergeant Parsons averred at the inquest that he had seen Clarke at 1 am as the sergeant was making his way between the Three Wantz and 'The Cottages'. So according to Parsons Clarke was then at the right place at the right time and should have returned to the Four Wantz two hours later. The sergeant testified that he was there then, awaiting the rendezvous, but the lad did not show up. He said that he did not know what to think – had the young constable sneaked off back home to mother in Bedfordshire? Or become involved in a serious misdemeanor? Might he have had an accident – say breaking a leg – and was he lying helpless somewhere? But as the sergeant had other patrols to oversee, he could only return to the Dagenham police station and report the fact that K313 had not made his rendezvous. There the matter rested until the other constables reported in at 6 am on Tuesday morning. PC Clarke was not among them.

Now all ranks became alarmed. A report was put in to K Division headquarters. Since he was not in his lodgings a letter was sent straight away to his widowed mother's home in Battlesden, near Woburn, to see if he had made his way there for some reason. How worried that good lady must have been as she wrote back that he definitely was not there. Now PC Clarke was pronounced officially 'missing' and, suspecting that he had been the victim of foul play, the police began dragging the ponds and other stretches of water in and around the village of Dagenham, of which there were many. Men were out all day on Wednesday, Thursday and Friday searching fruitlessly until they came to the farmhouse where the Page family lived. When PC Kimpton asked Mrs Page if the police could drag the ponds on their land she gave them permission, said there were two ponds, and told her two sons to show them the way. William Page, the older boy, described later how, in the evening of a beautiful, cloudless day, 3rd July, he took them to the second pond, via a potato field belonging to neighbouring farmer Collier – and so they made the awful discovery.

George Clarke was only 20, he had been in the police only a very short time, and barely a month at Dagenham. Yet in that time he had made a good connection with the villagers, and the police were more than satisfied with his attitude, his steadiness and his performance. On this particular beat he was following in the footsteps of Constable Abia Butfoy on nightly patrols from the Four Wantz, extending as was stated at the time: '. . . a considerable distance along unfrequented roads, having deep ditches on either side, covered with duckweed, some parts of the beat being extremely lonely . . .'

The actual spot where the corpse was discovered was about a quarter of a mile away from what was then the main road to Romford and roughly the same distance from the nearest point on the constable's official beat; giving rise to the idea that he had been drawn away from the road in pursuit of some miscreant, and there where he died George Clarke must have put up a tremendous fight against several men. The corn had been trodden down in a circle some twelve yards in diameter and there were spots and splashes of blood scattered all around. There is not much doubt that George Clarke had managed to defend himself initially and that some of his assailants were even then bearing obvious injuries. George was a well set up young man, and with his cutlass and his staff perfectly able to defend himself against a single attacker.

A local reporter suggested, 'From the appearance of the staff and the cutlass it would seem that the deceased was deprived of the former weapon early in the contest with his assailants, and that, finding it used against him, he had defended himself with his cutlass until he received a dreadful blow on the front of the head, which was

The village of Dagenham in 1889. *(Bennet Bamford)*

cut to the bone, and by which he was deprived of his senses'. On Saturday, the day after the discovery, the murder was reported to the magistrates at Ilford Petty Sessions. They directed the police to 'use every vigilance in their power for the capture of the murderers'. The newspaper claimed that the many policemen walking beats in rural districts were not allowed to carry firearms, although their comrades on horse patrol were. This case proved that such constables should now be armed.

The next stage in the story was the inquest before coroner C.C. Lewis and a jury, held at 2 pm on the following Saturday afternoon in a cottage close to the Three Wantz and within a short distance of the ruined house where the body was still lying. The awful nature of the injuries to the young policeman, and the fact that he was an officer of the law brought a great crowd of people around the cottage to hear the proceedings and see the notabilities. First, though, the coroner had to lead the jury through the crowd and along the road to the place where the body so sadly lay. The jury looked at those pathetic remains: '.... the sight was so horrid a one, that the mere

32

cursory glance taken of them was sufficient to render several persons completely heartsick'.

They all returned to the makeshift inquest room and the coroner opened the enquiry. The first person to give evidence was Constable K340 Thomas Kimpton. He recounted how he and George Clarke set out with the two other constables on a pleasant July evening to be marched off to their beats. George Clarke was sent westward and Kimpton went to the east. Those were the last minutes Clarke was seen alive. It was Kimpton who claimed to have made the discovery of the body after being alerted by the awful smell of putrefaction, then, he said '. . . looking about me, I saw the constable's staff I now produce lying in the ditch, and which I knew as soon as I looked at it to have belonged to the deceased'. The jury examined it, covered as it was in dried blood and much battered. 'I then went a little further, and discovered this cutlass sticking up to the hilt in the hedge.' The jury cast their eyes over it in horror. 'It was smeared with blood from the very point to the hilt, as if it had been completely passed through the body... About half a dozen yards from the spot where I found the cutlass I discovered the body of the deceased. He was lying on his back among the wheat, about three or four yards from the ditch. His legs were crossed one over the other, and his right hand was tightly grasping a handful of wheat.'

Then Constable K140 Abia Butfoy stepped forward to back up Kimpton's evidence. He passed to the jury the name of the person most strongly suspected by the police through their dealings with the criminal fraternity of the Dagenham and Romford area, but requested that it might not be made public at that time because such action would be likely to 'defeat the ends of justice'. Butfoy said that prior to 15th May 1846 he had been walking the beat subsequently taken over by George Clarke, and on the 4th March he had stopped 'a notoriously bad character from Romford' and ordered him to open his bag. He refused, a scuffle ensued and he was forced to show its contents. There was nothing suspicious therein. He said in farewell: 'I'll be at one with you for this!' It is possible that because of the darkness of the night he took out his revenge on the wrong man.

Then it was the turn of Sergeant William Parsons. The only additional information he could supply was that he had searched the dead man's clothing and found his policeman's rattle in his greatcoat pocket in such a position that he could not have reached it to sound an alarm. But there was, after all, very little chance of a member of the public hearing it in that isolated place in the middle of the night. He detailed the horrific wounds on the body and said that on that very morning he had visited the site again and found, 'Some pieces of the skull were so imbedded in the earth that I was compelled to use a knife to cut them out'. He gave his opinion that George had been decoyed to that field expressly for the purpose of murdering him. The surgeon, Mr J. Collins from Romford, was then called to detail all the wounds in the goriest detail. The coroner, thinking that an arrest was in the offing, then adjourned the inquest for a fortnight. The saddest event of this day was that George's mother asked to see her son's body. The coroner tried to persuade her against it. She was tearfully adamant. They took her to the ruined house, she gave one look at the mangled corpse – and passed out on the spot.

Two of Scotland Yard's recently formed detective force were sent to Dagenham to lead the search for the murderers. They made little headway. The search was extended to Romford and to all the surrounding villages. Every public house and beershop was checked for any criminal characters showing the wounds which PC Clarke must have inflicted as he sold his life dearly. Their efforts were in vain. Theories circulating locally were that he died through mistaken identity. It was PC K140 Butfoy who had trodden this beat regularly before George Clarke, and it was Butfoy upon whom the criminals of the area intended to be revenged for his zeal in bringing them to justice.

An interesting link in the subsequent unusual happening is that the local paper heard from Mrs Page, on whose land the body had been found but who had not been at the inquest. She told the paper that, living close by the scene of the murder, about three in the morning she had been woken up by the violent barking of her dogs in the yard, and fearing an intruder she had listened intently for any activity around the house. Then it was that she thought she heard a cry for help, though the continual barking prevented her hearing any other sound. But it was what she had to say at the resumed inquest on 22nd September which really put the cat among the pigeons.

She took the court back to midnight on 3rd July. The policemen had borrowed her husband's cart to take the body of George Clarke across the fields to the ruined house. 'I gave them some supper when they returned it, and whilst they were eating I asked Constable Kimpton where his sergeant saw the deceased last, and he answered, "To tell you the truth, Mrs Page, I did not see Clarke that night after he went on duty; my sergeant was very poorly, and asked me to do his duty, and I took his horse and went and did his duty for him".' The coroner thought there was something sinister here, someone had lied – why? Further enquiries were set in hand. As a result, though the murder remained unsolved, Thomas Kimpton, harness-maker turned policeman and Isaac Hicton, policeman and currier, were brought before the court in the middle of July 1847 to answer a charge of wilful and corrupt perjury. Hicton had stated that he had started his beat one hour earlier than Clarke, was supposed to meet him at about a quarter to midnight but Clarke did not turn up.

The coroner explained the circumstances of his first inquest and read out the statement made to him by Kimpton, and that made by Sergeant Parsons which agreed with it. He told how he had questioned Kimpton at the adjourned inquest when Kimpton swore on oath that he did not discharge the duty for Parsons on that fateful 29th June nor did he ever tell Mrs Page that he had. Mrs Page was then asked to repeat her evidence given to the coroner. The defence had brought forward John Stevens, quoted simply as 'one of the parties at the supper' who in fact was another policeman. He said he heard no such conversation, but Mrs Page's daughter came forward to support, under oath, her mother's veracity. Then, reported the *Chronicle*, Thomas Archer, a labourer on the Four Wantz Farm told the court, 'I was looking after my horses, when I heard a whistle, and just before two o'clock Kimpton came up to the gate, *on horseback*, and I gave him a light for his pipe. He asked whether I had seen Clarke, and rode on'.

Now PC Butfoy took the stand to say that he remembered talking with Kimpton about what had happened at the inquest. He did not know where Parsons was that night but Kimpton did say that he had done the sergeant's duty that night and, not seeing Clarke at the rendezvous, had traced his beat without success, returning just before daylight. Kimpton later told Butfoy, 'The evidence must be kept from the wrong hands, or they would see that it was false'. Another policeman in on the secret was told by Kimpton, 'If we don't keep to the statement we've made we shall get into trouble!' Apparently Parsons had made out a statement for his men to follow in their evidence to the coroner. Butfoy agreed, but after Mrs Page's statement he had 'blown the gaff'.

Hicton was then put in the dock. He had nobody to defend him. He told a familiar story of bullying by a superior officer. 'My Lord, we screened the sergeant in the neglect of his duty, and told a falsehood, not knowing the consequences; the sergeants make a report and have us turned out of our situations if we do not say what they please to order.' Butfoy was recalled; he confirmed this state of affairs and said that the cause of all their troubles was that Parsons had neglected his duty.

The jury found both Hicton and Kimpton guilty of wilful and corrupt perjury, though in Hicton's case they added their recommendation to mercy. On the following morning the judge pronounced sentence: both men were to be fined one shilling, imprisoned for one week and then transported to the colonies for a term of seven years. The inquest, having been adjourned several times pending further enquiries, including those into the behaviour of the police in general and the sergeant, Parsons, in particular, had to be closed with the verdict 'Wilful murder by person or persons unknown'. PC Butfoy could not live with his conscience. He went off, without permission, to the Commissioner of Police in London and told him of the perjury by him and his colleagues at Dagenham during the inquest. There was a further examination of Parsons and the constables and they were all put under arrest, close arrest in Parsons' case.

Rumours now flew around that George Clarke had been killed by his own comrades because he was so conscientious in his duties and religious in his private life. He had discovered his fellow policemen and the sergeant were colluding in some grave offence and they felt they must close his mouth for good. So, the rumour went, the ambush was arranged and the sergeant used his rank to get the murdered man led into a place far from public eyes.

Parsons came increasingly under suspicion of malpractice at the station, but further enquiries elicited no new information. The men were released from their arrest but all were dismissed from the police force.

Twelve years later, when the horror of the murder had been tempered by time and overtaken by crimes which, by their very number, crowded out its memory, a drunken woman told three female friends what may well have been the truth. She had been at the scene when five men had killed George Clarke, three of whom had since died violent deaths through, she said, divine retribution. One of the remaining men, George Blewitt, was arrested, but the police could get no corroborative evidence. Though Blewitt's case was forwarded to the next assizes it was not proceeded with, he was released, and so the great Dagenham mystery remains unsolved.

5

THE BITER BIT

THE KILLING OF ABRAHAM GREEN AT STRETHALL,
FEBRUARY 1849

Sixty years ago the village of Strethall had its own entry in Kelly's
Directory of Essex. It listed just one 'Private Resident'—Lady
Herbert, and just one 'Commercial' concern—Strethall Hall Farm.
Even then, in comparatively modern times, it was an isolated place
on the very border of Essex with Cambridgeshire. The only building
of any note is the parish church, dedicated to St Mary the Virgin,
built by the Saxons and fully restored in 1868. A short distance from
it is Strethall Hall, and there in 1849 lived Nehemiah Perry, known
as 'an opulent and highly respectable landowner and occupier', his
brother Thomas and their housekeeper, Rebecca Nash.

The Perry brothers farmed the whole parish and employed most
of the population which totalled no more than a score. None of them
lived within shouting distance of the Hall which, but for the church,
was truly isolated. The brothers were over 60 years old – a good age
in those times of limited medical knowledge. Any burglar who knew
these facts would have seen the place as a fruitful source of booty on
a dark night with help so far from hand. So it was not surprising that
a gang of villains who were known to be operating over the general
area of the Essex and Cambridgeshire border should eventually light
on this spot for one of their raids. Fred Feather in one of his *Essex
Police History Notebooks*, gives us the details of the police presence in
that corner of the county in 1849: '. . . the area had its own policeman,
Constable 55 William Miller of Elmdon. At nearby Newport was the
Essex Constabulary Divisional station and its commander
Superintendent John Clarke. There was no inspector and sergeants
would not be invented for another six years. The largest local town
was Saffron Walden . . .' A glance at a modern map will show what
a large area PC Miller was expected to cover, day and night.

He was nowhere near Strethall on the night of Wednesday 28th
February 1849, when snow blanketed the sounds of movement and
winter held the house in its icy grip. The three inhabitants of the Hall

Strethall Hall and church. *(Essex Police Museum)*

had been driven to the comparative warmth of their beds by ten
o'clock that night. Nehemiah Perry woke up at about one o'clock in
the morning; what was that noise which disturbed him? It would be
another four hours before the horsekeeper put in his appearance.
Nehemiah described the noise later as 'a sort of smash' which stood
out from the usual sounds made by the wind in the nooks and
crannies, the windows and doors of the old place. He lay for a
moment trying to identify that noise – he had been woken more
than once by the jangle and rattle of the bars across the back door
when the wind got up. Suddenly there was another noise like the
sound of plates dropping and breaking into smithereens. Someone
was in the house; in their stealthy fumblings they must have knocked
down the plate rack to have caused such a crash.

Nehemiah was out of his bed in a flash and had grabbed the gun
he always kept loaded at his bedside for just such an emergency.
Even as he took it up he heard an inner door burst open from a heavy
blow. He went out on to the landing, flung open his brother's door
and woke him with the cry, 'Halloo, Master Thomas, here's something up!' Thomas did not take long to size up the situation, grab his
gun, and join his brother on the landing, where they cleared the

cobwebs of sleep, shivered in the dead of that snowy night, listened apprehensively and tried to penetrate the darkness that gathered round the foot of the stairs.

What a clamour suddenly burst out; it seemed like nine or ten men at least, yelling and screaming at the top of their voices. One phrase they picked out: 'Go to it you bugger, we are all right now, go on'. They were encouraging a man who was coming along the passage to the foot of the stairs with a lantern in his left hand and what appeared, in its glimmer, to be a pistol in his right hand. To prevent recognition he seemed to have a scarf or some material over his face, secured beneath his hat. The brothers saw him turn as if to come up the stairs. Nehemiah was a man of mettle, he coolly took aim and fired. The man fell like a log, his back against the wall. To his brother Nehemiah said, 'Don't be frightened, there's one all right; I've snuffed his candle for him.' Then they heard another man call out for the shot man's pistol, but none of the gang dared to put themselves within range of the brothers' guns. All went very quiet – the burglars melted away – they were climbing out of the window. Nehemiah challenged them: 'Ha! ha! ha! there's cowards, why don't you come on like men.'

Rebecca Nash, the housekeeper, no spring chicken herself, in her own bedroom had heard the first noises, so she struck a light and got up straight away. When she heard the report of Nehemiah's gun she opened her door to see what was amiss – but was told to get back and close her door. Agitated, fearful, she walked to and fro, waiting for reassurance, but her master could not yet give it her. He and his brother stayed out there on the landing waiting, watching, listening with their fingers on the triggers of their guns, and getting colder by the minute. Nehemiah very much feared that the would-be robbers had laid an ambush and were keeping still as mice to lure him down the stairs to his death, or to his capture as a hostage to be traded for cash and valuables. So while Rebecca alternately sat in the warm nest of her bedclothes, or looked out of the window on to the white landscape for any sign of movement in this frightening drama, the two men stayed out on the landing, taking it in turn to grab what warmer clothing they could. In their situation four hours passed very slowly indeed.

At about 5 am noises told them William Walker, their faithful horsekeeper, had arrived from his home at Littlebury Green to go in the stables and start work. Nehemiah opened his bedroom window and called the man over. 'Some people have been breaking into the house, and we have killed one man at the bottom of the stairs, and you must go round the house to see where they have got in.' William bravely made a tour of the outside of the house and found the parlour window where the men had broken in. Meanwhile the three of them had dared to come downstairs and let him in by the door from the brewhouse. They all looked round as the light of day, aided by the snow's reflection, slowly seeped in. At the foot of the stairs they found a heavy bludgeon, but the man they had shot was not there. They found that the gang had dragged him in to the room they always called 'Old-Hall Parlour'. He was dead as a doornail. One of his mates had unbuttoned his waistcoat and pulled up his shirt to see how badly he had been injured, to find a horrible huge wound in his chest. It showed them all the futility of trying to carry him away as they made their escape. The sacking covering his face had been

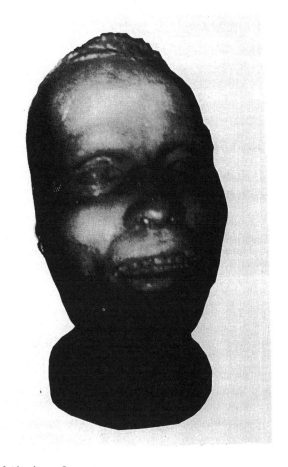

Death mask of Abraham Green.

pulled up above his nose, perhaps in the hope that he would answer their questions.

Under the window in that room another bludgeon had been abandoned. Outside, in the snow under that same window the gang had left a flurry of footmarks, but all so overlaid that, apart from guessing that they had been made by four or five people, no individual prints could be picked out. The window itself had been broken open, the frame eased out to remove panes of glass. The next step Nehemiah took was to send William Walker to knock up one of the villagers and send to Elmdon for the policeman.

Constable William Miller was soon on the scene. Summoned at six o'clock on that Thursday morning, he made haste straightway to the Hall. They were glad to put it all into his hands, showing him the dead burglar, the smashed window and the broken plates from the rack still lying on the floor. By then Nehemiah, his brother and Rebecca must have been too tired to pick up a plate. PC Miller saw the jumbled footprints, went some distance out from the house and was able to distinguish four separate sets of blurred footprints. He set out to follow them towards and round the hamlet of Catmere End; a footpath runs that way today. But the burglars had put too much distance between them and the constable to make a longer pursuit feasible, with a dead man still in the house.

For such a serious crime as shooting a man in cold blood, a man who, in fact, had not fired his own weapon against the Perrys, it was necessary to call in the top man at the divisional police headquarters. Superintendent Clarke was at the Hall by 9 am and started his investigation as soon as he had received his constable's report. First he searched the pockets of the dead man, finding only a meerschaum pipe, 13s 8d in cash, an unusual pair of pliers and a knife of the sort carried by most labouring men at that time. Clarke reckoned he had seen his face before, as recently as three or four days ago, along the Cambridge road between Chesterford and Newport. He suspected that it was a face 'familiar to the officers of police in every direction', but none could put a name to it.

The whole story had to be told again at the inquest on the dead man, held at the very place in which he had died – Strethall Hall, on Saturday, 4th March. The dead man lay exactly as his friends had left him on the floor. The coroner was C.C. Lewis and he had 'a highly respectable jury of agriculturists, of whom E.L. Bewsher of Littlebury was chosen as foreman. The dead man still remained unidentified. The coroner heard evidence from the Perrys and their housekeeper and the police. Then he told the jury that the facts were 'so exceedingly clear, plain and simple' that he need hardly say more. If they were satisfied that Mr Perry's life and property were in peril after the house had been burglariously broken into, as it evidently was, it was his duty to tell them that their verdict would be justifiable homicide, for it was clear that where a man's life and property were in danger he was perfectly justified in shooting any man so endangering them.

After that direction the jury took no time at all to further consider the case – they wholeheartedly and unanimously agreed with the coroner's expressed verdict. The latter then took the unusual step of drawing up a formal, legally worded record that 'Mr Nehemiah Perry, in doing what he had done, had lawfully acted for the protection of the life of himself and others'. Then the foreman of the jury stood up to make a little speech. 'Gentlemen, I think that, after first acknowledging our thanks to a kind Providence that Messrs Perry and their household have been thus mercifully preserved, it is our bounden duty to express our high opinion of the coolness, the intrepid conduct, and the indomitable courage displayed by Mr Perry and his brother under such trying circumstances; and I am sure that all would agree with me that they are entitled to the thanks of the jury, their neighbours, and their countrymen, and we all rejoice that Mr Nehemiah Perry is still in the land of the living, which it was too evident it was the intention of these wicked men that he should not be, and I hope that he will live long to enjoy the property he possesses and the respect of his friends.' Quite a speech for an inquest in a village deep in the heart of Essex with a population of just 20 souls!

But the business was not quite finished. One of the jurymen, a Mr Robinson of Littlebury, was able to add a little detail. He produced a pair of crudely made 'overshoes' and showed them round. One of his workmen had found them in a field which lay athwart the route the burglars had taken after the shooting. They were fashioned from an old cloth waistcoat and tied over a man's boots with string to deaden the noise they might have made creeping up to the Hall.

The dead man had used another ruse, he had pulled on an additional pair of stockings over boots and all. The curious thing was that both items had bits of barley chaff clinging to them. PC Miller, at the trial, attested that, in tracing footsteps in the snow, he noted the men had stopped near the barn where piles of barley chaff remained after threshing, and in the barley chaff there were signs that people had sat down. This was where the gang had stopped to pull on the stockings and overshoes on their way in.

At that time no one could identify the dead man or connect him with any other criminals known in the area. It was not for lack of trying; literally hundreds of people, more sightseers than possible informants, had passed through the parlour to look at the dead man as he lay on the floor. A newspaper reporter seemed to enjoy this unusual assignment: 'His countenance is of a very forbidding kind, and his head bears a general resemblance to that of Daniel Good, who was hung for murder some time ago in London. Some silver and several false keys were found in his pocket. He appears to be about 30 years of age; 5ft 4in in height; sallow complexion, dark hair, the whiskers appear to have been worn large, but have recently been very closely trimmed, and left very narrow; he appears to have been quite clean shaven within a short time of his death. His right eye-tooth is out. He had on a white shirt, black-and-white neckerchief, one white cotton stocking, blucher boots tied in three holes, cord trousers, drab cloth double-breasted waistcoat, stout blue cloth coat with pockets inside, black Paris hat, apparently bought at Peterborough; a large pair of worsted stockings were drawn over his shoes, and this plan seems to have been adopted by the whole of the gang.'

After the inquest and by the special dispensation of the coroner, Superintendent Clarke was allowed to keep the body unburied as long as possible to seek its identification, so it was put in an open coffin which was kept in the church belfry, where the cold weather helped to keep it in reasonable condition. The identification was not long in coming. A Cambridge policeman came over and said he was sure the corpse was that of Abraham Green, a well-known poacher and petty criminal from Dalham in Suffolk. Previous terms in gaol meant that various identifying marks on his body had already been noted in gaol books. He used the alias Woods and was often called 'Little Abel' by his partners-in-crime. With that information to go on, it was not long before two men who had been known to keep company with him were brought into Newport police station and closely examined in the presence of a magistrate, the Hon. C.C. Neville. They were William Goody, 21 years old, living in Halstead, but with a reputation for evil-doing in Chelmsford, and William Palmer, 26, a hawker, off his usual patch at Ashby-de-la-Zouch. Palmer had been arrested when he was spotted running towards Strethall on the very day that the Superintendent and two policemen were taking Goody to Newport.

Nehemiah Perry went to the hearing and said he definitely recognised Goody as the suspicious-looking fellow seen near his house, for no apparent reason, some three weeks previously. He had also seen another man who stuck out as a stranger in that isolated place, but he could not say on oath that it was Palmer.

The clinching evidence was that of Benjamin Taylor, chief constable of Peterborough. He came down to identify Green and added that he knew the two men now held were Green's associates.

Superintendent Clarke asked for more time to produce further evidence against the men, so they were remanded in custody until Monday 12th March. At the next examination of the prisoners before four magistrates at Newport police station further proof of their implication in the plot was forthcoming. Superintendent Barnes of the Hertfordshire police caused Goody to be taken to Strethall Hall and played a trick on him. He had Green's body taken out of the coffin and 'placed in an upright position, in a corner of the room, with his hat on, and on the prisoner's arrival, he was placed by his side; no one could have known but that he was alive, as his eyes were open; I then asked Goody if he knew the man; he turned round to him, and said, "No, no, I never saw him before in my life" – the prisoner evidently strove to prevent his emotion, which was very plain, as he could scarcely get the words out ... '

At the hearing clothing which Goody had been carrying in a bundle was shown to Palmer, who said it all belonged to him. Amongst the items were some very wet boots and stockings, of the same kind that Abraham Green had used to cover his boots, and there was some of that barley chaff still clinging to them. The men's movements on the night in question were outlined by the keeper of a lodging house at Barnwell near Cambridge who saw their return in the morning.

At the very last moment after the hearing finished with the men being committed to prison for trial at the assizes, and when two of the magistrates had already left, William Palmer asked if he could see the two remaining and, over the next two hours, he made a complete confession, giving all the details of the expedition and its inglorious end. He stoutly maintained that Goody had nothing whatsoever to do with it and named the other men involved. Nevertheless both he and Goody had to stay in gaol until the trial could be arranged. At the assizes in July 1849 the judge directed that the jury should acquit Goody on a technical fault in the framing of the charge against him. Palmer went to gaol for 18 months. There is no record of the other miscreants ever being brought to justice. One might say that by his death Abraham Green paid the price for their freedom.

His end was certainly inglorious. Nehemiah Perry was allowed to keep the body. He, according to Fred Feather, packed it into a game basket and sent it to a Cambridge surgeon who was later to become Sir George Paget, with the brief note: 'Dear Dr Paget, I have shot a burglar. N. Perry'. The papers had made such a sensation of it that he hardly needed to say more. A Mr Ward of Saffron Walden had already made a death mask of the murdered man. A cast from the mould can still be seen in the museum at Saffron Walden.

6

FAMILY TENSIONS

THE MURDER OF JOSEPH LEATHERDALE AT SALCOTT,
DECEMBER 1890

A hundred years ago the tiny village of Salcott was a bleak and desolate place, on the road to absolutely nowhere. The sea crept in across dank mudflats. In winter the east wind whined through leafless, stunted trees – small wonder the Reverend S. Baring-Gould chose it as the scene for his depressing, melodramatic Victorian novel *Mehalah* – 'a weird, grim tale of the marshes'. Kelly's 1891 Directory of Essex shows none of those more wealthy 'Private Residents', says 'The land is held by small owners', and the only tradesmen or commercial people listed are one publican, at the Rising Sun, one shopkeeper, one thatcher, one miller and three farmers of whom we particularly note Joseph Leatherdale. The directory was therefore out of date before it was published for, in December 1890, that man was dead – murdered and flung in a cupboard.

What a turmoil it caused in that village, how the rumours ran around, from shop to pub and back again. Everybody knew Joseph Leatherdale, he was 69, had lived in Vine Cottage, down the narrow lane opposite the Rising Sun for nearly 20 years, and before that he had been landlord of the White Hart inn at Virley just across the creek. Recently, in addition to farming, he had been making a few extra shillings a week as a carrier, driving his horse-van regularly to Colchester and back. It was through the summer of 1890 that he had been troubled by a strange outbreak of vandalism and graffiti on his farm.

Around Easter time he had gone into the stable and found that someone had cut off his horse's tail, a mean and senseless thing to do, for it left the horse defenceless against the flies which plagued it through the summer. The next aggravation was a message chalked on the stable door: 'You'd better be on the look out I have not done with you. I shall cut the horse's tongue out and shoot you and Arthur if you do not mind out'. Then a new message appeared: 'If you stop long you will have hell' with a kind of afterthought: ' – and you shan't

45

stop long'. This was followed by the appearance of a propped-up board on which was scrawled 'I hate the very sight of you in Salcott'. Then the vandal moved on to more risky doings – starting small fires in some of the outhouses in the yard which, luckily, were soon discovered and doused.

These manifestations of someone's slightly crazed anger and frustration were, by villagers-who-knew, as we might put it, attributed to 'Arthur' himself, who was 17, and lived with his uncle at the farm. The illegitimate son of Joseph's sister, now living in South Africa, he was an awkward teenager and there was no love lost between the two. A few days before Christmas 1890, when Joseph Leatherdale met Mr Strutt, who lived at Maldon but had a farm at Salcott, they talked about the world in general and then Joseph's nephew in particular. 'Well, I don't know squire,' said Joseph, 'but this 'ere young 'un is going to be a trouble to me. He ain't a drunkard, but he will get out of a night with the girls. I count he will get himself into trouble, and then go and enlist for a soldier. He's a rum 'un.'

On Saturday morning, 27th December 1890, Arthur got out the trap and horse to take a neighbour to Colchester market, and also offered his best friend, a lad named Foakes, and his mother, now Mrs Moss, a day's outing. They had what would have been called in those days 'a regular spree', he spent an awful lot of money, and on the way back they called in at a pub and he stood them a quartern of spirits each, a quarter of a pint in our reckoning, and that was not something a young village labourer could do every day. Mrs Moss kept a small shop on the village street, and in the course of the day Arthur asked her if he could lodge with her for a few days because his uncle had gone off for a holiday. With the two lads being such friends she could hardly refuse.

On the following Monday Arthur decided he would visit his cousin, Mrs Kezia Sortwell, Joseph Leatherdale's last surviving daughter, who lived at Tollesbury and worked for Dr Salter as a nurse in his practice at Tolleshunt D'Arcy. Arthur told his cousin that her father, his uncle, had gone to London for a holiday. He then handed her a half sovereign, saying that uncle had asked him to take it to her as a Christmas-box and to tell her that as far as the pudding and the cake she had made for him, well, she could eat them herself. Mrs Sortwell knew very well the strained relationship between the old man and the feckless youth. She really did not think that her father would make any communication at all to her through him, let alone trust him with a golden half-sovereign. It must have been feminine intuition, although we might now also call it Arthur's 'body language' which told her there was something strange in his behaviour. She asked him how her father had set out for London. He

Two further paintings by Jack Bridge. *(Essex Police Museum)*

said that he had walked to Kelvedon station in his high hat and with a change of clothes. She was moved to ask Arthur if his uncle was in his right mind. Arthur replied, 'He appeared so', adding that Joseph had taken the key of the best beer and wine with him, but that he, Arthur, would tap another cask they had in the house; if his uncle could go off to enjoy himself at Christmas, Arthur would make sure he also enjoyed himself. When Kezia asked him what he was going to do for money till uncle returned Arthur told her he had been given ten shillings for his board and five shillings for the horse to be clipped – 'and I shall earn more'. His uncle had told him he would write when he intended to return so Arthur could make sure the bed was aired.

Arthur seemed so truculent and vague about his uncle's movements that suspicion mounted in Mrs Sortwell's mind. She telegraphed her father's two brothers at Wakes Colne and Kelvedon, to see if Joseph was with either of them, only to get two curt replies of 'Have not seen him'. The next step she took was to walk up to Tolleshunt D'Arcy to confide all her worries in the local bobby, PC Birch. She told him she did not believe her father would leave home all of a sudden like that, and as for going to London she exclaimed, 'He wouldn't know where to go!' PC Birch was the right man for the job. Even though it was now nine o'clock at night he set off with Kezia to Salcott, where he had the good sense to call first on a trustworthy man who lived at Salcott mill, Charlie Smith and his son Arthur. All four of them headed for the Mosses house where Arthur was lodging. They were not invited in; Arthur came to the door and, when asked if he had the key to his uncle's house, said he had not but knew where to find it.

Now there were five of them going to Joseph's house, Vine Cottage, where, in the darkness Arthur groped his way to the back of the brewhouse, only to come back saying, 'It's not there, perhaps the little boy Foakes knows where it is – I'll go and fetch it.' By 10 pm he was back, gave them the key and provided an oil lamp. While he waited downstairs, the other four looked round the one bedroom upstairs. They found nothing at all to confirm their suspicions. But when they came down again, with just one flickering light, they could make out Arthur lying flat on the floor in the passage between the two downstairs rooms. He cried out, 'Ooh! Ooh!' as if in pain. PC Birch asked him 'Have you hurt yourself?', thinking the lad had fainted and fallen, but he got no reply. They all moved into the back room, the kitchen. On the way the constable had spotted the cupboard under the stairs with a bench propped against it and a sack of grain upon it. He pulled the door open just a little and saw – a foot! A human foot! He cried out agitatedly, 'Here he is! Here he is!' He then asked Arthur, now recovered, to come and look, to confirm it was his uncle. The door was dragged wide open, but Arthur would not look in – was it fright, or guilt?

The others all saw, eerily illuminated, Joseph Leatherdale, lying on his back with his head right at the back of the cupboard and his legs seemingly stuffed in either side of the door. The view in the lamplight was sickening. Someone had wrapped a sack around his head, and it was covered in congealed blood. It had been tied around his neck with a halter. Charles Smith was the first to speak, 'This is just what I thought must have happened.' At that moment Arthur Leatherdale broke in, hurriedly, excitedly, 'I was here when he was shot, I helped to put him in the cupboard. There were four or five others here with me at the time'. Before the policeman could get a word in, Charles Smith interjected, 'Who were they?' Arthur Leatherdale replied, in quavering bravado, 'I won't split; I'll take it all myself.'

He did not say another word as PC Birch went through the necessary routine for taking him into custody on suspicion of having killed his uncle. The night was far advanced when PC Hawkins turned up to lend a hand. Together they lifted Joseph's body out of the cupboard, while Arthur just stood there. Even in the poor lamplight they could see the dreadful gunshot wound in the back of the head. When Constable Birch asked Arthur where the gun was he said, 'It isn't here', but as the lamp was swung round, the constable had noticed a couple of shotguns in a corner of the kitchen by the back door. That detail would have to wait, it was time to take Arthur Leatherdale, as the prime suspect, into the custody of Superintendent Ackers at the Colchester police station. They did not get there until half-past one in the morning. Spare a thought for a most distressed and sorrowing Kezia Sortwell who, somewhere about midnight, was making her solitary way back to Tollesbury – a cold and lonely journey after a desolating discovery.

Arthur Leatherdale was brought back from Colchester police station to face coroner and jury at the inquest held on Christmas Eve at the Sun Inn. The whole court made a careful inspection of Vine Cottage and its grounds. One by one the jury viewed the body now lying beside the cupboard under the stairs, by the light of a candle and an oil lamp, a truly ghastly experience. They saw the dried blood on the stairs and the wall. It was Jonathan, Joseph's brother from Kelvedon, who officially identified the body. Arthur Leatherdale was made to stand in the room while this was going on. He had dressed himself neatly enough in a long coat with a cape over his best suit, but he could not meet the gaze of any man present. He fixed his eyes on one spot, and remained dumb. Only once was his inner concern shown, when he burst into tears. But was he feeling sorry for himself, or for the fate of his uncle? We shall never know.

Dr A.W. James, who worked for Dr Salter, reported on his examination of the corpse. He had found an almost circular hole where the neck joined the skull, big enough to put a finger in. For two inches round it the hair was singed and the skin discoloured, as it would have been by gunpowder. The inquest was adjourned until the following Tuesday and young Leatherdale was taken back to Colchester, where he was to be officially charged with murder. Prior to appearing before the magistrates, however, he asked to speak to Sergeant Creasy: 'I can't say what I've got to say before all them there in the room; I should like to write down what I have to say.' He was provided with a pen and paper but warned that what he wrote could be used in evidence. He persisted in his request and set out the following statement:

'I did not kill my uncle, but I got someone. I told him all the money he had got in his pockets he should have for the job, and he got some more to help him, and after they had shot him I gave them a sack and a halter. This is all I have got to say, and I shall not split.

24th Dec., 1890 [Signed] A. Leatherdale.'

On the following Monday Joseph Leatherdale's remains were

buried in Salcott churchyard at 2 pm in a coffin of elm with black fittings and the inscription 'Joseph Leatherdale, died Dec. 20th, aged 68 years'. A snowstorm blew away the words of the clergyman and edged the black-coated mourners in white. Blinds and curtains throughout the village were closed in respect. Mourners had paid their last respects to the dead man as he lay in the open coffin in his house. One of them reported that his face wore such a peaceful expression. From what the experts said he had known no fear or pain, death was sudden and instantaneous, he had not even known there was a man with a gun behind him. Mourners included his daughter Kezia and his brothers Jonathan and Elias. Kezia was so obviously broken-hearted at the graveside that even bystanders were moved to tears. There was a police presence unusual for those days – Superintendent Ackers, four constables, and some men quietly attending in plain clothes.

Next morning the adjourned inquest was reopened in the Salcott schoolroom. The suspect remained in custody. Kezia told her story again – it was like a nightmare taking on reality. The lies that boy had told her! She repeated his story that his uncle had gone away, leaving him money for his keep and for the horse being clipped, that Joseph would write before his return so that his bed could be aired. He even had the gall to tell her that if he heard from his uncle before she did he would let her know, while in fact his uncle's body was already stiffening in that cupboard.

Kezia then had to explain to the coroner and jury that Arthur's attitude to his uncle had not been violent in any way. Joseph Leatherdale had found that the boy was running wild, had become an inveterate liar. He threatened to report him to the police after his last foolish escapade. Joseph had gone down to Tollesbury to see his daughter because he had missed money, cheques and household goods. Could she do her best to trace the receivers with whom the boy was involved? It was too late, but he did tell Kezia that should he die unexpectedly, she was to look for what little money he had left in a white box hidden under one of the bricks which made up the floor.

On Christmas Day itself surgeon Arthur James and Doctor Salter made a post-mortem examination of Joseph Leatherdale but they were able to add little to the information obtained by the police in their examination and their conclusions as to the weapon used and the closeness at which it was fired. There were no marks of violence other than the single gunshot wound. They found 105 pellets from the shot lodged in the base of the brain. The possibility of suicide was absolutely and positively ruled out. The absence of blood spilled in great quantity was explained by the fact that from such a wound, in such a place, blood would not spurt out.

At the inquest Mrs Mary Caney came forward to say that she had seen Joseph alive at Vine Cottage at about a quarter to nine on the morning of 20th December. She had wanted to take some produce to sell in Colchester market, and he was the carrier. It was Arthur who actually opened the door and told her his uncle would be going at half-past nine. But it was only Arthur who called, close on ten o'clock, to tell her that his uncle was going to Kelvedon, but he would take her. They stopped at Layer Breton to have the horse 'roughed' or trimmed while Arthur had a drink of rum and cloves. He appeared generally in good spirits. She remembered that at about nine o'clock she had heard a gun going off – dull and muffled as if in a confined space – somewhere along the village street. William Cullen, a labourer, told the court he thought the noise came from the direction of Vine Cottage. He did not tie it up with Arthur Leatherdale because he was in such a good humour the following day having brought back for him, from Colchester, a cigar and an orange, generosity he had never shown in his life before! Mrs Moss then came forward to tell her story of that same journey to Colchester: 'He was more lively than ever I have seen the boy before. He was "talkified" all the way to Colchester, laughing and chatting . . . while in Colchester . . . he asked if he could come to my house to sleep. I said "Yes", and returned with him from Colchester. On reaching Salcott he went to the farmhouse to look after the horse, and came to mine about half-past eight. He never breathed his uncle's name except than when he came in to tea he told me his uncle had gone out to spend Christmas. He stopped with me from the Saturday night until he was arrested.' Her son, Arthur Foakes, aged 18, said he had slept with him from Saturday until the evening of his arrest and he did not appear in the least disturbed, day or night.

Superintendent Ackers had some incriminating evidence to put forward: 'I found upon the prisoner 18 gun caps, a purse containing two half-sovereigns, two half-crowns, one florin and one shilling, two keys, a watch chain and compass attached, three receipted bills, and the broken screw end of a ramrod, which corresponds exactly with the ramrod of the big gun found in the house of the deceased. I proceeded at once to Salcot . . . and made a thorough examination of the house. In the kitchen I found the two guns, the smaller one being loaded. The large one appeared to have been recently discharged . . . On the 26th I received a sample of shot and caps from a Mrs Lawrence of Salcott who sold some to the prisoner, and these correspond with those taken from the loaded gun.'

So the inquest closed with the jury pronouncing a verdict of wilful murder against Arthur Leatherdale. The next step in the sorry story was his appearance before the magistrates at Colchester and his commitment by them for trial at the Assizes at Chelmsford in March. The chairman of the bench closed with the remark, 'Superintendent Ackers and the police constables acting under his directions deserve the greatest credit for the way in which they have brought this case before the court.'

After three months in gaol, Arthur Leatherdale, now 18, went into the dock at Chelmsford on 11th March 1891. He was no longer the brave, cocksure fellow who had been throwing his money about in Colchester. He answered 'Not guilty' to the charge but for the rest of the trial, said an onlooker, 'He sat in the dock with his head hanging down on his chest and his hands on his knees, and seemed as much dead as alive, and almost unconscious of what was proceeding.' One interesting fact was brought out for the first time, Kezia Sortwell said she had relatives on her parents' side who were deaf-mute, one of whom was in the Brentwood Lunatic Asylum, while her own father's father 'was not quite the thing.' Arthur, also, was thought to be a not very sharp lad, 'believed at times to be rather wanting,' a very strange boy whose father, 'Crazy Charlie' Barrett, now dead, had paid Joseph Leatherdale £100 to bring him up as his own. Medical opinion brought before the court, however, was that Arthur Leatherdale was entirely fit mentally and certainly capable of distinguishing right from wrong, and the gaol surgeon gave the opinion that the prisoner was responsible for his actions from the time he first saw him in prison. The prosecution summed up: 'The probable motive of the crime was to get the old man's money and to spend it in the way the prisoner wished, and possibly to gratify a certain feeling of vindictiveness.' The defence counsel tried a direct attack on the publicity the case had received: 'This was one of those cases where the great misfortune came in of having everything published previously in the newspapers. No trial could come on without a jury being already acquainted with the facts, and this often prevailed upon their minds in the consideration of a case.' The second line of defence was to put forward the plea of insanity.

The judge summed up and the jury needed but 40 minutes to pronounce their verdict of 'Guilty – with a strong recommendation to mercy on account of his youth.' Arthur Leatherdale said not a word. The judge then put on the black cap and pronounced the sentence of death by hanging. In a matter of days the Home Secretary had commuted that sentence to life imprisonment. For 20 years Arthur Leatherdale served his time of repentance and Salcott forgot all about him. When he was released on 11th June 1911 aged 38 years neither national nor local newspapers noted the event and Arthur Leatherdale followed his uncle into obscurity.

7

THE SOBER,
EDUCATED
PHILANDERER

THE MURDER OF FLORENCE DENNIS AT PRITTLEWELL,
JUNE 1894

The *Essex County Chronicle* of 29th June 1894 was fairly buzzing with the news that shortly after six o'clock on the previous Monday the body of a young woman had been found in the brook at Prittlewell, the village which became the heart of Southend-on-Sea. But it was not a case of drowning – there was no more than an inch of water in the little stream. Close examination showed the poor woman had been shot in the head.

The actual spot was in the fields behind the vicarage, about three quarters of a mile from Prittlewell bridge westwards along the footpath following the course of the brook from Prittlewell bridge. Footpath and brook have gone now, lost in a maze of streets off Prince Avenue, where Colemans Avenue reminds us of Coleman's Farm, and Southbourne and Westbourne Groves keep the memory of the 'bourne' – the Prittlewell brook which in those days ran on through Springfield. It fell to the unfortunate Mr Rush of Royal Crescent, Southend, to make the horrifying discovery. He had been to Coleman's Farm on business and was coming back along the footpath when he spotted a glove dropped by some lady who, he may have thought, would be cross when she arrived home without it; but almost immediately he came upon the sickening sight of gouts of congealed blood and then the heart-wrenching sight of the body of a woman in the stream a few feet below the path.

The body had been cast down from the footpath so violently that the head had made a depression in the soft bed of the stream. One

A sketch of Inspector Marden made during the Moat Farm trial. As a sergeant he recovered the body of Florence Dennis *(Essex Police Museum)*

gloved hand was bent over the body and a leg twisted beneath it. Mr Rush gazed with dismay at the cloud of blood which made a halo round the head in the almost stagnant water. Then the urgency of the situation struck him and in his haste to get help he rushed straight past the Prittlewell police station and on down to the Southend station where he gasped out his story.

Sergeant Marden calmed him down, carefully noted the facts, then called together a number of constables and set out for the brook, picking up the Prittlewell man, PC Webster, on the way. They were as shocked as their informant at the grim sight, but it was their job to remove the body from public gaze to the privacy of a room in the Spread Eagle Inn to await the inquest. This they did using a sheep hurdle. Though it was clear the girl had been shot, an initial search of the area did not discover the weapon that had been used.

The identity of the victim was soon established. She was Miss Florence Dennis, 23 years old, and in advanced pregnancy. She hailed from London and had come down to stay with her sister Mrs Ayriss, whose husband was manager of the Express Dairy Company's branch in Southend. Florence had been a lively young lady. She had a job in London but still lived at home with her mother and father, a harness-maker. Further investigation showed that on Sunday evening she was seen walking and talking with a man on their way from the railway station along North Street and past the Blue Boar. The police told excited reporters that when Florence was found she was wearing a dark double-breasted jacket. It was still properly buttoned as she lay there and her other clothes were undisturbed, but her straw hat lay on her breast. The cause of death was all too evident – a bullet hole in the temple.

Mrs Ayriss heard of her sister's death in the most shocking way. Because of visitors she had arranged that Florence was to sleep at a neighbour's house on Sunday night but she had not arrived there nor returned to her sister's house the next day. Mrs Ayriss was so worried that she went to the police station on Monday evening to ask for their help. There and then she was told the awful truth. After recovering from the shock, Mrs Ayriss was able to reveal that Florence had set out on Sunday to meet her sweetheart, a paymaster at the London docks, at the railway station. The police followed this up and found someone who had seen a couple similar to the description at ten o'clock at night walking in the direction of the spot where the body was found. With Mrs Ayriss to help it did not take them much time to establish that Florence, some two years before, had met and fallen for the charms of James Canham Read who, unbeknown to her, already had a wife and eight children in Stepney. It was only very late in her pregnancy that Florence had found out this fact. It made her so depressed that she threatened Read with the publication of her plight and his deception, for his wife knew nothing of their relationship. So matters came to a head when Read had a telegram sent to Florence at her sister's address fixing up a meeting.

Then various witnesses attested to seeing the couple walking within half a mile of the fateful spot and that the man was trying to persuade the unfortunate girl to walk further on across the dark and lonely fields. From other statements in the subsequent trial it appears that Read, whose youngest child was only 15 months old, had seduced Mrs Ayriss before transferring his affections to her sister Florence. What is more he was also dallying with a Miss Kempton of Mitcham. So it seems James Read was the architect of his own downfall through his reckless philandering.

A hundred years ago becoming pregnant outside marriage was considered highly immoral – even the newspaper had to use the term 'enceinte' to denote that Florence was in an advanced state of pregnancy. She certainly needed urgently some assurance from her lover that she and her baby would be living with him in future respectability. That assurance had not materialised and now Florence lay like a rag doll, flung in the brook with a bullet through her head. While hundreds of people walked out from Southend just to stand about at the scene of the murder, the police were much more active. Having heard from Florence's sister, Mrs Ayriss, their interest centred on James Canham Read.

He was believed to have spent Sunday night in the area of Southend simply because the last train to London had left before he could get back across the fields. Enquiries in London revealed that he arrived at his dockyard office at 10 am on Monday, explaining that he was delayed through having to visit a fellow clerk at his home before starting work. On that Monday afternoon, before going to the police, Mrs Ayriss had sent Read a telegram at his place of work asking him if Florence was with him in London. Read's mind was still working well – he immediately wrote a reply and posted it straight away, declaring his surprise at such an inquiry, 'as I have not seen Florence for eighteen months'. By four o'clock he had left the office, and nobody knew where he was. On Tuesday, in his absence, his accounts were examined. It was found that at least £150 was missing, along with certain papers. A further revelation was that for at least three weeks Read had been in possession of a revolver which he kept in a drawer at home. That was sufficient to tip the scales in favour of an urgent search for the man. Inspector Reid of the CID, working with Acting-Sergeant Fenner of Southend police issued a warrant for the arrest of James Canham Read, including the facts that he was about 39 years of age, 5ft 5ins in height, of medium build 'with a slight bend and gentlemanly appearance, fresh complexion, slight, light brown moustaches, fine full eyes'. When he was last seen he was dressed in a black coat and vest (ie waistcoat), light grey trousers, and wearing a brown hard felt hat. The description concludes, 'He is sober, educated and intelligent, and of exemplary character'.

While the search went on for the suspect the jury, as they say, 'sat on the body' – in other words the coroner's inquest on Florence's death was held at the Spread Eagle Inn, Prittlewell, where the body lay. The local and the docks police were represented. Police Sergeant Marden of Southend said that he had gone with Frederick Rush to Springfield field on Barlands Farm and found the body lying in the centre of the brook, on its back, dead and cold; 'Her head was inclined to the left side in a pool of blood'. The grass was flattened from the footpath to the brink, but there were no footprints in the mud at the bottom of the brook. A large clot of blood on the footpath and a bullet wound just above the left ear were mute evidence of the cause of the poor girl's terrible death.

Mrs Ayriss, who had been brought to the Spread Eagle to identify the body was very affected. Between tears she outlined Florence's situation, saying Florence had put two telegrams, unsigned, in her pocket, but they were not found on the body. She knew that Florence met the sender of those telegrams on two occasions. From the first, on Saturday, she had come back bright and hopeful, saying she was to meet her lover again. She had agreed to see him again at 9 pm at the Great Eastern Railway Station at Prittlewell. From this assignation she never returned. Mrs Ayriss had gone to the station at

WILFUL MURDER

WANTED

For the Murder of Florence Dennis at
Southend-on-Sea, 24th June. 1894

JAMES CANHAM READ

Cashier, Royal Albert Docks. London.

Age 39. Height 5ft 7in,
Hair Brown,
Moustache Slight Brown,
Small Side Whiskers,
Eyes Brown and prominent,
Complexion Fresh.
Two Upper Front Teeth
project slightly,
One overlaps the other.

DRESS,
Dark Brown Hard Felt Hat,
Short Black Coat and Vest,
Light Grey Trousers,
Walks Quickly,
Is of very smart and
Gentlemanly appearance.

Has a Gold Watch engraved inside case " Presented
to Mr. James Canham Read by his fellow Clerks, Royal
Albert Docks, London."

WARRANT ISSUED.

Information to be sent to
SUPT. HAWTREE, Southend-on-Sea.

FRANCIS & SONS, Printers. &c., 65, High Street, Southend and Rochford.

The poster which was quickly issued by police.

this time, with or without her sister is not clear, but she said that she definitely saw Read there. She claimed that she recognised him because when she lived at St John's Hill, Wandsworth, he was courting Florence and she saw them together many times. The fact that a much closer relationship had existed between Read and Mrs Ayriss came out during the trial.

Dr Waters made the post-mortem examination. He reported that there were no external marks of violence other than the bullet wound. The bullet was found 'in the substance of the brain'. From the state of the wound he judged that the gun must have been held very close to Florence's head. One man who had interesting information to give the police was Mr Dowthwaite, the Prittlewell umbrella maker. He was passing the entrance to the footpath across the fields around 10 pm when he heard a man trying to persuade a woman to take that path. Mr Dowthwaite's description of the man was very close to that the police already had of James Canham Read. But for the moment Mr Read could not be found. PC Fenner had been looking for him in the London area on Tuesday and Wednesday without success, ever since he had left his docks office taking with him a large sum of his employers' money.

Ports were watched and sightings were claimed from Sheerness to Southampton, but in the capable hands of Inspector Baker of the CID the whereabouts of the philanderer was soon established – the clue which clinched it was that young lady of Mitcham. 'I went to the neighbourhood of Mitcham on the 7th July,' the Inspector was to tell the court on the third day of the trial. 'I knocked at the door of Rose Cottage. A woman came out, and while I was in conversation with her the prisoner came out of the house and, taking part in the conversation, pointed across the green and said, "If you want Mr Young [the owner of the cottage] he has gone across there, you will be able to catch him up." I said to him, "James Canham Read?" He said, "No". I said to him, "I am an inspector of police. I shall arrest you as being James Canham Read, for the murder of Florence Dennis . . . " ' Inspector Baker then took the man back into the house and searched him.

He found Read was in possession of the large sum of £48.10s in gold and also of the cutting from a national newspaper concerning the inquest on Florence Dennis. In his pocket there were keys which fitted the safes at the Albert Docks. Clothes found in the house were of the same style and colours as witnessed on the night of the murder – and in the trousers there was a special revolver pocket. What is more, no less than £35 in silver was found wrapped in towels and pushed under a bed. The inspector took Read back through London to Southend Police Station where he was officially charged with 'feloniously, wilfully, and of malice aforethought, killing and murdering Florence Dennis, at Prittlewell, on 24th June, 1894'.

Florence's funeral had taken place at St John's church, Southend on 30th June, followed by interment in the churchyard. Her father was absent, her mother was so upset that 'her grief was sometimes terrible to witness'. She had to be supported on each side by a son and daughter as she looked again on the coffin with its single wreath and its plate inscribed, 'Nothing in my hand I bring, simply to Thy Cross I cling. Florence Dennis, died June 24, 1894, aged twenty-three years'. When the coffin had been lowered into the grave Mrs Dennis's children said, 'Take one last look, mother'. She bent over, cried 'Florrie, Florrie, Florrie!' and fell back in a deep faint.

When Read's trial came on in November, the county newspapers were full of it, issuing supplements to cover it in detail. The pressmen of Essex filled the press gallery in Chelmsford's Shire Hall while London reporters and newspaper artists had to find seats in the body of the court. James Read was brought down from the prison on Springfield Hill in a cab as early as 6 am 'so as to avoid anything like a scene' and held in a cell at the Shire Hall. It was a drizzling miserable morning when the court began to fill just after 10 am, but that did not keep crowds of sightseers away. One eye-witness tells us that: 'The only alteration from the appearance he presented at Southend was in the growth of a short dark brown beard and whiskers. Formerly he simply sported moustaches. He was wearing his suit of grey tweed and a white collar and small black bow tie, which, added to the fact that his waistcoat was unbuttoned halfway down, permitted the display of a good deal of shirt front, ornamented with pearl studs. All heads were bent forward to catch a glimpse of the man who was the central figure of one of the most sensational of recent murder trials.'

Read pleaded not guilty to the charge of murder, but guilty of the second charge of stealing £159.12s from the India Dock Joint Committee. Since it was obvious that the trial would be long, Read was allowed to sit in the dock, where he took notes assiduously. The Solicitor-General put the case for the Crown. He began by touching on the prisoner's career as a cashier at the Royal Albert Docks on £140 a year – a trusted employer over many years of the Dock Committee. He left without giving notice on 25th June 1894 and never returned. Then the prosecutor moved on to his private life, tracing his connection with Florence Dennis and her elder sister Mrs Ayriss. He had met the latter as far back as August 1889 and the acquaintance soon ripened into 'immoral relations'. In September 1890 the two of them spent a night together at Leigh, near Prittlewell. In the same month Florence was staying with her sister at Wandsworth and was introduced to James Read for the first time. He remained intimate with Mrs Ayriss down to March 1892, writing to her frequently as 'Mrs Neville' at an accommodation address in the same road, St John's Hill Road, as that in which she lived.

In May 1892 Florence left her parents' home to stay with her sister, who was having a baby, probably by Read. It was then she wrote two letters to Read at his office address. A witness was to say that she was 'absent from her sister's house until late one Saturday night' – she too had fallen under the philanderer's spell. He wrote back to her as 'Miss Latimer' at the same accommodation address. In later letters he re-christened her 'Louise Talbot' in a continuing relationship whilst she was staying with another sister in Sheerness.

A further complication was Read's meeting Miss Kempton on 16th October 1892. He told her he was Edgar Benson of Poplar and, by the spring of 1893 he had seduced her. As a man with a lawful wife and eight children, the man's sexual appetite seemed insatiable. Beatrice Kempton came from Cambridge but Read persuaded her to move to Hallingbury where she was installed as a kept woman. On 6th January 1894 she gave birth to a child and a month later he found her lodgings in Rose Cottage, Mitcham. Read accounted for his many absences by saying he was a commercial traveller.

The address at Poplar he had given Beatrice was his brother Harry's place of work. But that address had to be changed when Harry was dismissed for misconduct. By April 1894, when it was obvious that Florence was pregnant Read was worried and depressed – his pigeons were coming home to roost. He told Beatrice Kempton he was being 'pressed by creditors'. From Christmas 1893 to June 1894 Read spent only three Sundays away from Rose Cottage and his Beatrice. His lawful family just had to manage without him. After much pondering the matter of what to do about Florence was decided and put in train. Brother Harry Read was coerced into sending a telegram, in his handwriting, from the West Strand, London office on 23rd June, making an appointment to meet Florence the next day.

Now the Crown followed the movements of Florence on 24th June. She was then obviously pregnant, probably not wanted at home because of the scandal, and so living with her sister Mrs Ayriss in Wesley Road, Southend, in a house so full of family and lodgers that it was arranged that she should sleep that night at a neighbour's. She went out at about 9 pm to see someone, and she was never seen alive again. Read was also seen in the area before Florence had set out and, later, within a few yards of the spot where the body was found. A Mrs Kerby witnessed that he was there and asked her the way to Leigh – being told she did not know he said he would 'go back to

Rayleigh', and turned on his heel. Robert Dowthwaite also identified the prisoner as the man arm in arm with a woman as they walked up Gainsborough Avenue in the direction of the footpath to the scene of the murder. Richard Golding coming out of a public house, with his wife and daughter, saw a man and woman go up Gainsborough Avenue. Later they saw the man return alone and walk along the Leigh road. Constable Daniels early next morning, testified that he had seen the man Read at Benfleet, heading for London.

It transpired from further evidence that at just after nine on the morning of the next day an unusually dishevelled and unshaven James Read called at the house of a fellow clerk at Leytonstone, made himself presentable, and reached work just an hour later. It was shortly after this that he received Mrs Ayriss's telegram. He sent her that letter to stave off further enquiry, then panicked, took the money and headed out to Mitcham and his third mistress. On the way he sent a note to his brother Harry, 'Secure my desk's contents [at his home in Jamaica Street, Stepney] and return everything to me at M[itcham] in strict secrecy. Will explain all when I see you. Allay all fears'. As the Solicitor-General observed – 'That letter showed that there was important work to be done at Jamaica Street, and that important documents were to be destroyed.'

A really damning piece of evidence was a gun traced to the ownership of Harry Read. He had bought it from a Gravesend billiard-marker in a fit of depression after losing his job. It was a pin-fire revolver taking a No. 7 Eley cartridge and had been taken out of his possession by his brother James and his sister Mrs Kelly, because they did not feel they could trust him with it in his depressed state of mind. The type of bullet it fired was the same as that which killed Florence Dennis – and now the gun could not be found. PC Marden explained how he had gone to Mrs Kelly's address and received from her a box of the same pin-fire cartridges.

The trial went into a third day. A local reporter, having fought his way through the throng to his reserved seat, looked about him and planned his report: 'Again a change in the weather, but a day withal in keeping with the dread proceeding in court. The waters swell before a boisterous wind, which howls mournfully round the grey Shire Hall, adding a weird impressiveness to the scene. Mr Baron Pollock (the judge) again took his seat at ten o'clock and James Canham Read appeared in the dock. There was a marked change in the prisoner's appearance. He was paler and wore a very anxious look. He seemed occasionally to wander into dreamland, fixing his eyes on a certain spot, and remaining immovable. He maintained a composed attitude, however, sitting with his arms folded and legs crossed, and occasionally moving to make a note on the blue foolscap paper which he has always had with him.'

The defence called no witnesses and claimed the right to speak last, but the judge ruled that this was the indisputable right of the Solicitor-General in prosecuting. So the defence lawyer made the best of the case that he could, saying that the case had been so publicised that the jury could not bring unbiased minds to their deliberations, yet they must ' . . . dismiss any question of immorality with regard to the behaviour of the persons in this enquiry'. He tried to discount the evidence of Mrs Ayriss as largely perjury with the 'wicked intentions' she had towards Read. That was the best he could do. On the fourth day the prosecution put the case so forcibly that the jury took just 15 minutes to find Read guilty. Asked if he wished to say why sentence should not be passed upon him, Read repeated that he was perfectly innocent – had never seen Florence over the past two years, had never fired a revolver in his life and was 50 miles away at the time and the place of the murder.

The judge was visibly much moved as he pronounced the sentence of death by hanging. Upon receiving a request from the jury and considering the stress they had suffered in the course of the trial the judge discharged them all from further jury service until the end of the century. On Tuesday 4th December 1894 at 8 am the black flag was unfurled on the flagpost atop the gaol. 'There he goes' cried someone in the crowd which had gathered at the prison gates.

8

JUST A PAIR
OF BOOTS

THE MURDER OF CAMILLE HOLLAND AT QUENDON,
MAY 1899

Clavering is a very rural retreat between Newport and Saffron Walden, made up of scattered hamlets and the actual village. A lane on the right past the village leads to the hamlet of Starling Green – the nicest name for the location of the nastiest crime – murder!

There is nothing about Moat Farm today to even hint at the happenings of 95 years ago; but there are still some souvenirs of the tragedy to be seen in the Essex Police Museum at the police headquarters at Chelmsford, including a pair of boots. They are ladies' boots, I hasten to say, a pair of small, dainty boots in which the genteel Miss Camille Cecile Holland stepped so elegantly round the gardens of Moat Farm, Clavering, until she was cruelly murdered there in 1899. Stand in the lane outside the house today and the pastoral scene is so peaceful that the truth seems unacceptable, but let me give you the facts.

Miss Camille Holland, a lady of about 56 years of age was living, as so many maiden ladies did in those days, in a boarding house in London. She has been described as 'a rather pretty, faded, delicate-looking woman who took, to preserve her youthful appearance, means that were rarer in those days than they are now. She powdered her face, dyed her hair a reddish-gold, and was careful over all the details of her toilet; her landlady has left it on record that, though she looked about 60 in bed, when she was finally "got-up" for the day she seemed ten or fifteen years younger'. She was an intelligent and accomplished woman, educated at a school run by her aunt, who eventually retired to live in London with her. She was a woman devout in her faith in the Roman Catholic Church but, at the same time she did enjoy male company whilst remaining sexually innocent. To cut a long story short Camille's aunt died and left her

Camille Cecile Holland   Samuel Herbert Dougal

a fortune in invested money to the tune of some £7,000, a colossal sum at that time.

Enter Samuel Herbert Dougal, described as 'a cheerful anthropoid' with an animal magnetism. 'Men might dislike him, but they could not deny the fascination of his intense vitality.' He set himself to get on well with anybody who could be of use to him. At 20 he enlisted in the Royal Engineers and served for 21 years, earning promotion through the ranks and a good pension at the end of it. He was from the start a devil with the ladies. In 1869 he married; in 1885 his wife became suddenly ill and died on the same day. Two months later he had married again. Within two months that wife was taken suddenly ill and died. Since he was in English military quarters in Canada no questions were asked.

Two more women were inveigled into living with him in succession. By this time he had fathered seven children. After his discharge from the army he started living well above his income, and simply resorted to forgery to make up the difference. He was caught, sent to prison and lost his army pension. On his release he lived on his wits, cheating gullible young girls out of their miserable savings by his charm and his personable appearance. By the time he was 50 he had remarried and was literally down and out. Then came a stroke of good luck, he met Camille Holland. It is said that it was a chance encounter at the Earls Court Exhibition in 1898, but that cannot now be established, and another source claims that it was as a result of an advertisement in a 'lonely hearts' column in a newspaper.

How he worked his magic on this more than middle-aged lady we shall never know. Perhaps he offered, ostensibly, the affection and interest of which she had been starved for most of her life. He was still a fine-looking man, a proper man-of-the-world to whom she could look up, and perhaps be a little frightened of in a thrilling way. He persuaded her to buy a place of their own where they could settle down in cosy intimacy – Coldhams Farm, Quendon, near Clavering. It was Dougal who renamed it Moat Farm as more romantic-sounding. Miss Holland it was who insisted that it should be put in her name, much to Dougal's disgust. They took lodgings in Saffron Walden while work was being done on their love nest. Their landlady, Mrs Wisken, described how Dougal would come cycling back from Moat Farm and his supervision of the work in hand. He would start ringing his bell at the end of the street so that Camille, waiting in their rooms, would hear him in time to go to the front door and let him in. They exchanged kisses and he would put his arm around her and take her into their sitting room.

When the work was done the loving couple moved in. They said goodbye to Mrs Wisken on 27th April 1899 and, taking Camille's much loved little dog Jacko with them, they were driven over to Moat Farm in the trap by Henry Pilgrim who went with the house as it were. Mrs Wisken was sorry to see them go, they had seemed such a happy couple, and Miss Holland had taken her into her confidence in long talks together while the master was away. But Dougal could not resist the temptation to flirt with any woman who came within his orbit. Now that Camille was quite on her own at Moat Farm Dougal tried to force his attentions on the servant girls who came and went very quickly without giving the real reasons for their sudden departure. It was Florrie Havies who brought the problem out into the open. She took the greatest exception to Dougal's pawings and told her mistress of his crude attempt to kiss her the minute it happened. She would have left that day, but Camille begged her to stay, for she herself had become rather fearful of her 'husband's' behaviour, his threatening physical presence when roused. Florrie rather reluctantly agreed to stay on and Dougal, when tackled about it, was surprisingly calm and contrite.

Things seemed back to normal, then, on 16th May, Dougal tried to creep into Florrie's bedroom. She shouted for Camille, and another hysterical scene was played out, ending with the two ladies sleeping together for their safety. Yet, by 19th May husband and wife, as they liked to consider themselves, appeared to be as one again, planning to go into town to do some shopping. Did she mind, asked Camille of Florrie. No, Florrie did not mind, providing that Dougal went with her. They were only to be away for an hour or so. Camille waved, 'Goodbye, Florrie, I shan't be gone long.' Florence watched them drive away in the trap. She was the last known person apart from her killer to see Camille Holland alive.

It was not until eight o'clock in the evening that Dougal came back – on his own! The frightened Florrie asked, 'Where is the mistress?' 'Gone to London,' said Dougal in a matter of fact fashion. 'What,' cried Florrie, 'gone to London and left me here alone?' 'Never mind,' was the reply, 'she's coming back soon and I'm going to the station to meet her.' Florrie knew, through sheer common sense, that her mistress could not have got to London and return that same night, and here she was, cut off in this isolated house with that nauseating old man who would be sure to try something on. Several times Dougal went out between nine and just after midnight, telling Florrie that he was going to meet the mistress, but never came back with her. Then he told Florrie that Camille had not come back and that she had better go to bed. Dougal knew that Florrie had written to her mother, asking her to come on the morrow and take her away from this dreadful situation, so it was unlikely that he would make further advances to the 19 year old. Nevertheless Florrie took no chances, she crept from her bedroom to the spare room, locked the door and sat by the open window, ready to climb out if he were to break down the door. A long night's vigil ended when she heard the farmworkers arrive. She ventured downstairs, where Dougal told her, mildly, 'I've just had a letter from Mrs Dougal [it was too early for a letter to have arrived], she tells me she is staying on for a little holiday, and is going to send a lady friend down to look after the domestic side for me.'

Florence just waited for the moment her mother arrived around eleven o'clock, then rushed into her arms. Like a lioness Mrs Havies verbally attacked Dougal for his ungentlemanly behaviour towards her daughter. She demanded, at once, Florrie's month's wages and the fares for both of them, including the hired trap. He paid up immediately, banging it down on the kitchen table, muttered that he had done Florrie no harm, then drove off in his trap, leaving them standing there. They packed all Florrie's belongings and set off for Newport themselves. They passed Dougal, still on his own. He whipped up his horse to pass them at speed. Did he have something to hide?

He was not telling a lie about the 'lady friend' coming to join him; it was in fact his real wife for whom he had sent, and he met her at

Newport station with the trap on the very next day, 20th May. Deception was the order of the day. Having called Camille Mrs Dougal as they got to know society round about, he had to introduce his real wife as his daughter to a clergyman who called. Later Mrs Dougal confided to the clergyman's wife that she was Dougal's real wife, saying that Miss Holland was away on a yachting holiday and that she had said that she could do what she liked with the clothes she found in her wardrobe. So she took to wearing some herself and gave her confidante a nice black shawl.

Not much time passed before Dougal found a way to avoid time and energy spent on the farm and its produce. He had all the documents necessary to get access to Camille Holland's savings and investments. He wrote a letter to the Piccadilly branch of the National Provincial Bank saying, 'Miss C. C. Holland presents her compliments to the manager, and will be glad if he will forward her a new cheque book'. On 6th June Dougal sent to the bank a cheque made out to himself and also asked for £30 to be sent in £5 notes. The bank queried the signature of Miss Holland, which he had, of course, forged, and asked for confirmation by a further signature. On 8th June it received another clever forgery with the note:

The Moat Farm.

' . . . Cheque to Mr Dougal quite correct. Owing to a sprained hand there may be some discrepancy in some of my cheques lately signed. Yours truly, Camille C. Holland'. Now life went well for Dougal. While the memory of Camille Holland faded from the minds of local acquaintances Dougal was signing her name to withdrawals from her share and bank accounts and placing the sums obtained in his personal account. He even had Moat Farm transferred to his sole ownership by correspondence. Nobody thought to ask where Miss Holland was. They presumed letters were in her hand, and her signature, forged, yet witnessed by Dougal, was sufficient authority.

By November he had let the farm go to the dogs. All the land by then had been laid down to hay, just a few domestic animals, mainly cows and pigs were kept for the sake of appearances. In that month he had tried, unsuccessfully, to sell the farm off altogether. He was having a great time. With plenty of money and time to indulge in socialising he made himself popular in the neighbourhood. He even gave £10 towards the Clavering church clock installed in commemoration of Edward VII's coronation. At home he was having his way with one servant girl after another; in fact it was common gossip by now that he was fornicating with a woman and her three daughters over the same period! After many a noisy row the real Mrs Dougal left in January 1902, to live with a labourer named Killick. In January 1903 an affiliation order against Dougal brought further gossip about the man and his amours, his failure to divorce his wife because of his own misbehaviour, and the strange disappearance of his mistress Camille Holland who had never even sent for, let alone come to collect all her clothes and other personal effects.

The local constable, James Drew, was so much concerned with the strength of feeling personally expressed to him that he took the unusual step of writing a letter to his Superintendent Barnard:

'Sir,

I have the honour to report, for your information that there is a talk in the Village Clavering about Mr. Herbert Samuel Dougal of Moat House Farm Clavering since last October a Detective named Giles was about Clavering Making enquiries respecting Mr Dougal and a Miss Holland, which thought to have been Dougal['s] wife, but about 4 years ago Mr. Dougal['s] wife lived at Stansted as his Daughter and Mr. Dougal lived at Saffron Walden till he came to the Moat House Farm Clavering with Miss Holland. After a time Miss Holland was missing. Mr. Dougal told People she had gone in the Continent and he was Expecting her back, but she has not been seen in Clavering since. Great many things are reported to be in Mr. Dougal's House marked C.C. Holland. Since the last two cases at the Bench from Moat House it roused people to talk again and it is now said it was Miss Hollands Money that bought Moat House Farm and People think now he must have done away with her and buried her. Dougal about 6 months ago applied for a Divorce from his wife who had misbehaved herself with a man Named George Killick Engine driver somewhere Nr. Maidstone in Kent and Dougal['s] wife Knows all about this affair of Miss Holland has threatened to split on him Killick has been heard to say there will be an Essex Mystery. Mr. Gaylor Farmer of Clavering was talking to me one day and his cows got into the old Castle Grounds he saw a Piece of Ground had been Moved the shape of a grave. I am told that letters has come to Moat House addressed Miss Holland and have been answered by Dougal's wife.

I have the honour to be, Sir,

Yours obedient Servant,

[signed] James Drew P.C. 124.'

The last two allegations proved to be quite untrue, but the whole letter serves to show the intense speculation being bandied about the area. The superintendent sent the letter on to Captain Showers the Chief Constable of Essex and he told the local man, Superintendent Pryke, to make a full enquiry into all these rumours. He found that Miss Holland's family had not heard from her since the beginning of 1889, but her solicitors and her bankers claimed that they had been in touch with her concerning her estate for the past four years. Miss Pittman of the Quendon post office said that over the period letters had been delivered to the Moat Farm, and taken from the postman at the gate by Dougal on most occasions.

Pryke then called on Dougal on 4th March, saying he wanted to see him with reference to the rumours going round the village concerning a Miss Camille Holland. Dougal bluffed as only he could, saying he had driven her to Stansted station some three years ago, with two bags of luggage and he had not seen her since. But when he went to the station Pryke found that no ticket for London had been issued at that date and time, according to the register still in use there. The CID had been called in and they checked some of the cheques involved on which the signatures could not be recognised by her family as those of Miss Holland. Dougal felt the police were getting too close for comfort after Pryke had called. The very next day he drew all the money he had, £605 from two banks, and set off for a weekend in London, followed by a weekend in a Bournemouth hotel with his latest paramour – another of his servant girls who was already pregnant by him. While she went back to the Moat Farm he stayed in London to change some of his £10 notes at the Bank of England. At that period these were high denomination notes and he did not realise how swiftly the police could act; they had already put

Miss Holland's body lying in the greenhouse before the inquest.

a stop on their acceptance. He was asked to sign one of them and give his address. Sydney Domville, he wrote, of Upper Terrace, Bournemouth. A detective very quickly appeared. 'That is not your name, your name is Dougal. These notes form part of the proceeds of a forgery, you will have to come with me.' On the way to the police station, almost there, Dougal made a dash for it, got well away, but without knowing it had run down a cul-de-sac! Taken a little more roughly and securely to the police station, he was thoroughly searched. The result was remarkable: 83 £5 notes, eight £10 notes, £63 in gold, a £5 gold coin and jewellery and two watches identified later as the property of Miss Holland.

With Dougal in custody an all-out search of the farmhouse and the gardens at Clavering was organised. He could not be held on the forgery charge for long, so the work went full speed ahead. Moat House was measured inside and out, walls were tapped for hidden cavities where a body might be concealed, floors and attics were scrupulously examined for hiding places – nothing was found. The digging of the garden to grave depth went on and on. Even the ancient moat was drained – to reveal nothing but a few fish gasping in the mud. The police were almost at their wits' end. If Dougal had disposed of his lover's body three or four years ago it was now going to be very difficult to prove. Then came their lucky break.

In the painstaking process of finding out just when Miss Holland had last been seen alive Dougal's farmworkers were closely questioned. One of them recalled that she had come to the farm on 18th May 1899. He remembered that precise date because it was the same day that Dougal had told him to fill in the open drainage ditch which, from time immemorial, had traversed the farmyard. This was the vital clue. Under the labourer's directions the ditch was excavated. Four hours of solid work went unrewarded. Eventually most of the ditch was dug out with absolutely no result. Then, suddenly, one of the diggers found a piece of cloth caught in the prongs of his fork. He stuck the fork into the soil again – and struck something hard. He brought the fork up, and on it was pinned a lady's small boot. The bones of the foot were still inside it. The riddle of Moat Farm was solved in that very moment of grisly revelation.

Further careful excavation revealed the body of a woman lying face downwards – or what remained of her after four years burial in Essex clay. Some portions of her clothing were well preserved because Dougal had crammed branches and twigs of blackthorn into spaces around the corpse in his hurried filling in of part of that ditch to bury his innocent and unoffending victim. Though poor Miss Holland had been so roughly bundled into eternity such a long time ago, a close examination of the remains of the skull revealed a bullet hole behind the right ear with an exit hole on the other side of the head. A fine thread of lead recovered from the area of the wound was conclusive evidence of the bullet which ended her life.

Measurements of the body tallied with the vital statistics recorded for Miss Holland. The clothing on the body was identified by Camille Holland's erstwhile landlady and, finally, the pair of boots found on the feet were identified by the bootmaker whose name was marked upon them. Miss Holland was understandably vain about her pretty little feet and the bootmaker was able to bring out her individual lasts to prove the point. So the police had the proof they needed to substantiate the claim that on or about 19th May 1899, when she was last seen alive, Camille Holland was murdered by Samuel Herbert Dougal. The forgery charge was dropped and Dougal was put on trial in the Shire Hall, Chelmsford, before Mr Justice Wright. The jury had no doubt, he was convicted of murder and subsequently hanged in Chelmsford Prison on 14th July 1903.

9

FOR THE LOVE
OF A LADY

THE MURDER OF PERCY THOMPSON AT ILFORD,
OCTOBER 1922

Filson Young, a well-known lawyer, once wrote: 'It may be that the present-day fashion of sensation-mongering in trials, and dishing up crime for the delectation of the Sunday morning lie-a-bed is to be reckoned among the less worthy of the uses to which the craft of writing can be put. Yet it is the public interest in justice which alone keeps it reasonably pure; and although we cannot all attend Courts of Law, we are all concerned in what is transacted there . . .' Seventy years later his words ring just as true. They were my encouragement in the researching and setting down of a murder at Ilford which was sensationalised from the day it hit the headlines to that early morning when justice was finally done.

It concerns but three main characters in a drama which quickly ran its course to a last act in a terrible crime of passion. What made this sordid example of a very common crime so newsworthy was the amazing number of letters read out in court and offered to the jury for their more detailed perusal. But for a couple of notes from the young male lover all these passionate letters were from the woman in this 'eternal triangle' and they made good reading in the newspapers on that Sunday morning in Ilford in 1922. Ilford then was a town growing into a large dormitory for the City of London just seven and a half miles away. Now for the characters.

Percy Thompson, born in 1890, was a shipping clerk in a city firm and by 1922 was earning a very respectable £6 a week. In 1916 he married an attractive intelligent girl called Edith Graydon who was ready to carry on with her own job so they could save for a house of their own. Percy was an inoffensive man without any markedly unpleasant characteristics, an ordinary fellow, perhaps a little dull in his settled habits and rather old-fashioned in his view of a wife as subservient to the husband. In the year of his marriage he was called to the colours to serve in the First World War, but within a few months he was back home again, discharged as medically unfit.

Edith was born in 1894 in Manor Park, a residential area a mile closer to London. She travelled daily to her job as manager and book-keeper of the millinery manufacturers Carlton and Prior in Aldersgate Street where she also took home £6 a week. In July 1920 they bought No. 41 Kensington Gardens, Ilford where they eased the burden of the mortgage by renting out a couple of rooms to a Mrs Fanny Lester. During the course of the trial Edith was described as '. . . the chief victim of her own tragic personality'; what was implied in that phrase? She was smeared and sneered at by the gutter press as a wicked married woman, already 28 years old when she corrupted a mere boy of 20 in her lust for love whilst living with a boring, weak and inoffensive husband. Yet a criminologist of standing, F. Tennyson Jesse, puts her in a very different light:

'. . . her passion for a prosperous and respectable union was so great that what she did apart from it, the way in which she spent her days, the way in which she amused herself, was of very little importance to her. She was capable of being a lively and amusing companion, and there are many humorous passages in her letters that suggest her intolerance of dullness, and the rather mischievous pleasure she took in shocking people . . . She was a very attractive woman, and in her business life she was extremely capable, and came constantly into contact with a large circle of acquaintances . . . and in the course of this independent existence she had many opportunities of amusement of which it is clear that she availed herself. It was a method of passing the time and speeding the hours of what was to her the unreal part of her life, as apart from the real dream-world she entered when she began to write to her lover. The profound sense of the triviality and unimportance of everything she did apart from him breathes through her accounts of dinners, dances, expeditions. It is this sense of proportion, so lacking in other ways, which gives the light touch to her little thumbnail sketches, full of wit and characterisation, of people that she met.'

In their efforts to smear Edith the media presented Frederick Bywaters as a manly young fellow, healthily innocent, bewitched, corrupted and debauched by the experienced woman of the world. An onlooker at the trial spoke of him as a good-looking, clean-cut and self-assured young man, aged 19 when he became involved with Edith. Up to that time he had been the greatest credit to his mother who had been widowed by the war. Mrs Bywaters on the witness stand slipped in that piece of the jigsaw which showed how her son made that fatal connection with Edith Thompson. As a lad he had gone to the same school as Edith's brothers, and he was also probably known to Percy Thompson, so a link had been forged.

At school he worked well, every report on him was marked 'excellent'; and this in spite of the fact that he must have been very upset when his father was killed shortly after volunteering for the army in December 1914. His father had been a ship's clerk and this must have influenced Frederick. When he left school he went into a shipping agents in Leadenhall Street, in the City. After nine months, and with another excellent character reference, he moved to a similar firm. It may be that he did not then go to sea because he knew his mother, having lost one member of the family, would not wish her 14 year old son to risk losing his life also whilst German battleships and submarines roamed the seas. In February 1918, as the war ground to a close, Frederick saw that he could join the merchant service in comparative safety.

So he found a berth as a ship's writer and followed in his father's footsteps on journeys all over the world, with just a fortnight's leave between return and sailing again. On every occasion he stayed at home with his mother and two sisters in Upper Norwood, even down to the last time he docked on SS *Morea*. The last time he was with his mother was on 4th October when he parted from her in St Paul's Churchyard just after 2 pm. When his mother was asked in court, 'Has he always been an excellent son?' she replied without hesitation, 'One of the best that a mother could have'.

Since his ship always docked at Tilbury there had been times when it was convenient for a night or two to lodge with the Graydons at Manor Park rather than in Upper Norwood. So it was that Frederick was able to further his friendship with Edith, now a married woman, as she and her husband visited her parents. He was also friendly with her sister Avis. In fact, it was as Avis's friend that he was invited to go on holiday in Shanklin, on the Isle of Wight, with Edith and Percy. Then it was that the match was set to the all-consuming fire of their romance. We hear, from one of the letters Edith wrote to her sweetheart: 'One year ago we went for that memorable ride round the island in the charabanc do you remember? Last night when I went to bed I kissed you goodnight in my mind because that was the first time you kissed me.' Frederick did actually ask her permission before he planted that first kiss on her tempting lips. He could not have guessed what the consequences would be.

Percy appeared to be totally unaware of the developing romance. He got on so well with Frederick that he invited him to return to their home with them and spend the rest of his shore leave there while he waited for another voyage. From 18th June until 1st August 1921 things went well between the three of them, though Mrs Lester,

The eternal triangle, from left to right: Frederick Bywaters, Percy Thompson and Edith Thompson.

the lodger, was able to say later that the Thompsons were not always on good terms, having heard them having 'very high words' at times. In conversation Mrs Thompson had told her that all the housework and cooking as well as her job and the necessary travel were getting too much for her, so she was going to employ a servant. That poor little servant-girl arrived to take up the job on the very evening after Percy Thompson was murdered! Mrs Lester also remembered a very interesting point; Mrs Thompson had shown her a nasty bruise on her arm, saying that the two men were arguing, and when she tried to come between them she was roughly pushed to one side and fell against the table.

The quarrel erupted on 1st August 1921, a Bank Holiday, when all three of them were in the garden, with Edith doing some sewing. She asked her husband to get her a pin, he refused, so Frederick volunteered to go indoors and get one. When he came back he detected a very strained atmosphere and guessed they had been having words. He might also have guessed, since that stolen kiss and other caresses, that he was the subject of the disagreement. After tea the bad feeling broke out again and, according to his account Edith was 'thrown across the room', overturning a chair in the process. Now Percy's feelings about the 'triangle' were brought out into the open. He ordered Frederick out of the house and he left forthwith, 'at Mr Thompson's request and my own inclination'.

He went back home to live until 9th September when he was back on board ship for another trip. But in that interim he had to admit that he was still seeing Edith from time to time and so much so that by the time his ship was due to set sail they were lovers, as we may gather from one of her letters: 'As I said last night, with you darling there can never be any pride to stand in the way – it melts in a great flame of love – I finished with pride Oh a long time ago – do you remember? when I came to you in your little room – after washing up.'

So the adulterous link was formed, so the die was cast. No doubt Frederick Bywaters was flattered by the attentions of such an attractive, clever, older woman who brought so much excitement to his intervals ashore. Edith Thompson seems to have lived two lives – one in reality with her dull and boring husband and her endlessly repeated work routine, the other in fantasy as the romantic lover and the tragic heroine of a drama where a handsome, much-travelled young sailor had come to take her away into a sunset of tempestuous romance. Before he left on his next voyage Frederick had agreed that he would write regularly to Edith, and in this way she was able to effect a subtle hold over his affections. He had not even left port when she wrote the significant note: 'Come and see me Monday lunch time, please darlint. He suspects.' All her letters to him were signed by his pet name for her – 'Peidi'. 'Darlint' was her shorthand for 'darlingest'.

Bywaters had kept all the letters she had written through the following year, 1922. They were largely the cause of the couple's ultimate fate. Many were read out in court as evidence of their conspiracy in murder. Most people and papers of the day thought she was a scarlet woman, depraved, a 'cradle-snatcher', but nobody listening to those epistles of love could deny that they were romantic literature of a moving quality. Reading between the lines one could also detect the way in which she was weaving a web of love around her 'victim' to bind him ever more closely to her as he came and went on his voyages. In the court they were quoted as 'A passionate and ardent correspondence . . . which showed that they were engaged, or intended to engage, in an intrigue'.

It was hard on Edith that she should have to endure the humiliation of the reading of such personal epistles in public for she had shown much greater discretion about the letters she had received from her sailor-boy. She writes, on 3rd January, 'Immediately I have received a second letter, I have destroyed the first and when I got the third I destroyed the second, and so on . . . ' Frederick was less circumspect. He may have been proud of the liaison he had made, reading those protestations of love again and again – or did he have other purposes at the back of his mind that made him keep all those passionate missives sent him by a married lady? One of the first letters she wrote to him on his outward journey contains passages which are the very stuff of romance. For instance:

'Last night I lay awake all night – thinking of you and of everything connected with you and me . . . I'll be feeling awfully miserable tonight darlint, I know you will be too, because you've only been gone one week out of 8 and even after 7 more have gone – I can't look forward, can you? Will you ever be able to teach me to swim and play tennis and everything else we thought of, on the sands in Cornwall? You remember that wonderful holiday we were going to have in '22, and that little flat in Chelsea that you were coming home to every time and that 'Tumble down nook' you were going to buy for me one day. They all seem myths now.' Do we suspect that there was an ulterior motive in Frederick's courting? It could be thought so from another sentence: 'I don't think I'll be able to buy that watch for you by Xmas, darlint, I'd like to ever so much, but as things are I'm afraid I can't afford to, but the will and the wish to give is there and I know you'll like that just as well.'

What young man, far away from England, home and beauty is going to resist such words as these: 'When I looked at you [i.e. his photograph] to say "good morning" an irresistable feeling overcame me, to put my fingers through your hair and I couldn't. I love doing that darlint, it feels so lovely – you don't mind do you? Most men don't like it, in fact they hate it, usually, but I know you're different from most men.' At the same time she chronicles her husband's failings. In that same long, long letter she writes '. . . he said I was fearfully strung up and feeling very morbid so you may guess this didn't improve things. However at night in bed the subject – or the object, the usual one, came up and I resisted because I didn't want him to touch me . . . He asked me why I wasn't happy now – what caused the unhappiness and I said I didn't feel unhappy, just indifferent, and he said I used to feel happy once. Well, I suppose I did, I suppose even I would have called it happiness, because I was content to let things just jog along, and not think, but that was before I knew what real happiness could be like, before I loved you darlint. Of course I did not tell him that but I did tell him that I didn't love him and he seemed astounded. He wants me to forgive and forget anything he has said or done in the past and start afresh and try to be happy again and want just him . . . These are his words I am quoting. I told him I didn't love him but that I would do my share to try and make him happy and contented. It was an easy way out of a lot of things to promise him this darlint.'

So Edith Thompson wooed her young lover Frederick Bywaters, tying him ever more closely to her and at the same time keeping her husband to the fore as the obstacle in the way of their ultimate happiness. Passages from these letters read out to the jury by the prosecution brought an intake of breath throughout the court, for they hinted darkly at criminal intentions. One, written on 10th February 1922, after Frederick had completed one voyage and left on another, said: 'You must do something this time – I'm not really impatient – but opportunities come and go by – they have to – because I'm helpless and I think and think and think – perhaps it will never come again . . . On Wednesday we had words – in bed – Oh you know darlint – over that same old subject and he said – it was all through you I'd altered . . .', a later paragraph declared 'It would be so easy darlint – if I had things – I do hope I shall'. Along with this letter there were no less than three newspaper cuttings. One spoke of the poisoning of a curate with hyoscine, the second was headed, 'Poisoned chocolates for University Chief' and the third, 'Beautiful dancer drugged'.

On 14th March she came out a little more directly with her pressure on her lover: 'I ask you again to think out all the plans and methods for me . . .' and encouragement with, 'I wait and wait so anxiously now – for the time when we'll be with each other even though it is only once – for "one little hour"'. It conjures up in the mind a vision of a silken web, baited with honeyed words. She sent other cuttings of a similar nature – one wonders just what she was conjuring up against her husband. During the long course of this correspondence we are hampered by the fact that she destroyed all but one of the letters she received. All the same, there was enough said in her letters to enable the prosecution in court after the awful event to point a very strong accusing finger. In her letter of 1st April she makes veiled references like this:

'I'm not going to try any more until you come back. I made up my mind about this last Thursday. He [her husband] was telling his mother, etc, the circumstances of my "Sunday morning escapade" and he puts great stress on the fact of the tea tasting bitter "as if something had been put in it" he says. Now I think whatever else I try it in again will still taste bitter – he will recognise it and be more suspicious still and if the quantity is still not successful – it will injure any chance I may have of trying when you come home.'

So, through a whole year the letters flowed to and fro, interspersed by those homecomings of the young sailor whom the married woman met at various rendezvous. In one letter a mystery is made of an hotel where they made love. The pattern of two months at sea and a fortnight at home continued down to 23rd September 1922 when Frederick came home for the last time. A year had passed since he had told his mother that Mrs Thompson was having a very unhappy life with her husband and had asked her how she could get a separation. Mrs Bywaters' disapproval of the affair was evident in her reply: 'There's no law which *compels* her to live with any man if she doesn't want to.' If only Frederick had thought over that commonsense statement he might have been able to escape that eventual fateful entanglement.

Passages like the following, from her letter of 1st May 1922 show the pressure being put on this brash but very inexperienced young man:

'About those fainting fits darlint, I don't really know what to say to you. I'm beginning to think it's the same as before – they always happen first thing in the morning – when I'm getting up, and I wasn't ill as I should have been last time, altho' I was a little – but not as usual. What shall I do about it darlint, if it is the same this month – please write and tell me, I want to do just as you would like. I still have the herbs.' Such circumlocution could be interpreted that she had missed a menstruation more than once through their lovemaking but had contrived early abortions with the use of a drug.

Another passage clearly shows her intentions:

'Wouldn't the stuff make small pills coated together with soap and dipped in liquorice powder – like Beechams – try while you're away . . . You tell me not to leave finger marks on the box – do you know I did not think of the box but I did think of the glass or cup whatever was used. Darlint, think for me, *do*. I do want to help. If you only knew how helpless and selfish I feel letting you do so much for me and I doing nothing for you. If ever we are lucky enough to be happy darlint I'll love you such a lot. I always show you how much I love you for all you do for me.' In that same letter Edith Thompson gives the screw of tension another subtle turn when she refers to his home-coming in a month's time:

'That month – I can't bear to think of it – a whole four weeks and things the same as they are now. All those days to live through for just one hour in each. All that lying and scheming and subterfuge to obtain one little hour in each day – when by right of nature and our love we should be together for all the 24 in every day. Darlint don't let it be – I can't bear it all this time – the pain gets too heavy to bear – heavier each day – but if things were different what a grand life we should start together . . . Do experiment with the pills while you are away – please darlint. No, we two – two halves – have not yet come to the end of our tether. Don't let us.'

These letters continue in the same vein, encouraging, imploring, too numerous to quote further. With all this tension and a heightened sense of his love for his mistress Frederick came back to England on Saturday 23rd September 1922 and stayed at his mother's flat. He went over to see Edith as soon as could possibly be arranged on Monday, when she finished work at 5.45 pm and took some refreshment with her in a nearby restaurant. He did the same on the next three evenings and on Friday took her out to lunch and met her again in the evening. On Saturday morning, telling her husband Percy that she had to work, she went walking with Frederick in Wanstead Park where he parted from her, reluctantly, at one o'clock. On the Monday, after the usual telephone call to her office Frederick took Edith to lunch and spent the afternoon with her until 6.45 pm. What plans were they making? Questioned later, Bywaters said that they were simply trying to get more resigned to the fact that Percy Thompson would never agree to a separation. With hindsight we might believe that they were planning a murder. Percy saw but one more dawn.

On Tuesday 3rd October Edith rang Frederick mid-morning as usual and they had lunch together at the Queen Anne Restaurant in Cheapside. Then he hung around so that he could see her again when she finished work and take her to Aldersgate Station at 5.30. She told him how fed up she was because she had to go to the theatre with her husband and her uncle and aunt, a long-standing arrangement.

But what plans had they laid for that very night?

Bywaters had an alibi prepared. That evening he went out to Edith's parents at Manor Park, to collect some tobacco Mr Graydon had promised him. He arrived about 6.30 pm and was still there at 11 pm. From that time Edith can take up the story as given in evidence in court:

'I spent the evening at the theatre, and came away with my husband. Leaving Ilford station with the 11.30 train from Liverpool Street, we walked along Belgrave Road. My husband and I were discussing going to a dance. I was trying to persuade him to take me to a dance a fortnight hence. When we got to Endsleigh Gardens a man rushed at me and knocked me aside. I was dazed. I do not remember anything about it, only being knocked aside. When I came to my senses I looked around for my husband, and saw him some distance down the road. He seemed to be scuffling with someone, and he fell up against me and said "Oo'er" ... I helped him along by the side of the wall, and I think he slid down the wall on to the pavement. I looked at him and thought he was hurt.'

She saw blood was coming from him. 'I went to get a doctor, and going along the road I met a lady and gentleman coming towards me. I do not remember what I said to them, but I know that we went to a doctor, and then I came back to my husband with them. The doctor was a long time in coming ... he said "He is dead".' Apparently, when Edith was taken back home early in the morning of 4th October she was under the impression that her husband was still alive, sobbing, 'They have taken him away from me: if they would let me go to him I could make him better'.

John Webber, a sales manager living at 59 De Vere Gardens said that he was on the point of going to bed about half past twelve on the morning of 4th October when he heard a woman's voice outside cry, 'Oh, don't, oh, don't' in a most piteous manner. He went into the street, found the man sitting up against the wall and was told a doctor had been sent for. He helped the doctor undress the man to make a closer inspection. He added that Mrs Thompson appeared almost hysterical.

Of course, the police were immediately notified. Their enquiries gained momentum as dawn broke and people began to go about their business. A locked box on Mrs Thompson's desk opened by the police contained personal letters. Was this the beginning of the trail to Frederick Bywaters? We now know that after the killing he returned home to Norwood, then travelled to London with his mother the next afternoon, bidding farewell to her at St Paul's Churchyard and then travelling to the home of the Graydons, Edith's parents. The police at the trial did not explain how they were alerted to visit the Graydons on the evening of 4th October, when they arrested Bywaters. Edith was also taken into custody.

The next morning, the 5th, a statement was taken from Mrs Thompson. At first she prevaricated, saying that she did not recognise Percy's assailant. Then, according to the statement of the Divisional Inspector, Richard Sellars, at the subsequent trial: 'I took her to the matron's room [at the police station]. In doing so we passed the library, where Bywaters was detained. She saw him . . . and said "Oh God, oh God, what can I do? Why did he do it? I did not want him to do it." She said, almost immediately after, "I must tell the truth." She was a little hysterical and I said, "You realise what you are saying, what you say may be used in evidence." ' She then proceeded to make a new statement, which again was written down and signed. It included three damning sentences ' . . . I saw my husband scuffling with a man. The man whom I know as Freddie Bywaters was running away. He was wearing a blue overcoat and a grey hat. I knew it was him although I did not see his face'.

Frederick had been taken to the station, asked to remove his coat, which was examined by a doctor, and then invited to make a formal statement. He claimed that he was never at the scene of the crime, but at a later interview on the evening of 5th October when the Inspector said, 'I am going to charge you and Mrs Thompson with the wilful murder of Percy Thompson', Frederick offered a further statement, including these facts:

' . . . on Tuesday night, 3rd October I left Manor Park [station] at 11 pm and proceeded to Ilford. I waited for Mrs Thompson and her husband. When near Endsleigh Gardens I pushed her to one side, also pushing him further up the street. I said to him, "You have got to separate from your wife." He said, "No." I said, "You will have to." We struggled. I took my knife from my pocket and we fought and he got the worst of it. Mrs Thompson must have been spellbound for I saw nothing of her during the fight. I ran away through Endsleigh Gardens, through Wanstead, Leytonstone and Stratford; got a taxi at Stratford to Aldgate, walked from there to Fenchurch Street, got another taxi to Thornton Heath. Then walked to Upper Norwood, arriving home about 3 am. The reason I fought with Thompson was because he never acted like a man to his wife. He always seemed several degrees lower than a snake. I loved her and could not go on seeing her leading that life . . . I only meant to injure him. I gave him an opportunity of standing up to me as a man but he wouldn't. I have had the knife for some time. I threw it down a drain when I was running through Endsleigh Gardens'. He later corrected himself over the knife, saying, ' . . . after I did it I ran forward along Belgrave Road towards Wanstead Park, turning up a road to the right. I am not sure whether it was Kensington Gardens where they lived or the next road. I then crossed over to the left side of the road, and just before I got to the top of Cranbrook Road end I put the knife down a drain; it should easily be found'. It was Detective Constable Hancock who found the knife, down a drain on the north side of Seymour Gardens.

As to all Edith's talk, in her letters, about poisoning and powdered glass it seems very unlikely indeed that she ever did any such thing. The senior pathologist at the Home Office, Dr Bernard Spilsbury, later knighted, examined the body of the murdered man and declared he could find no evidence of poisoning, or any scars produced by the passing of broken glass. Bywaters to the end declared Edith's innocence, saying that it was all a fantasy, 'she had been reading books,' and, 'She appeared to want to go away, but she used to get very hysterical. She was of a highly strung nature'.

Nevertheless, at the trial the Solicitor-General constantly referred to passages in her letters which could be interpreted as conspiracy to murder. When he questioned Frederick it gave the young man the chance to say that he had omitted to mention that Percy Thompson had in that assault threatened to shoot him – and only upon hearing that threat did he bring out his knife. Despite skilful speeches by counsel for defence of both man and woman the jury took only two hours to consider their verdict and found them both guilty. The death sentence was pronounced.

The judge had told the jury, 'The charge is simply and honestly, that of a wife and an adulterer murdering the husband', but it was that amazing series of letters read out in court which caught the public imagination and led to a great division of opinion in the newspapers as to whether Edith Thompson should have been found guilty. The person most deserving of sympathy was Frederick Bywaters' mother – she lost her husband in the war and her son to the clutches of a scheming married woman.

10

A DEAD MAN'S EYES

THE MURDER OF PC GEORGE GUTTERIDGE AT STAPLEFORD ABBOTTS,
SEPTEMBER 1927

People all over Essex heard the news on that new-fangled wireless, and read it in most of the dailies for that matter, but on Friday, 30th September 1927, they turned to their own local paper, the good old *Essex Chronicle*, to get all the details of a terrible tragedy which struck an Essex policeman's family. The *Chronicle* lived up to its reputation, reporting:

'One of the most remarkable crimes of recent years, claiming as its victim a popular Essex policeman, murdered in the actual performance of his duty, sent a wave of consternation over the county on Tuesday. While the countryside was still enshrouded in heavy early morning fog, Police Constable George William Gutteridge, aged 38, married with two young children, a member of the Essex Constabulary stationed at Stapleford Abbotts, was found foully done to death at Passingford Bridge, within 400 yards of his home at Townley Cottages, Stapleford Abbotts. At first there was a suggestion that an accident had happened – that the policeman had been knocked down by a passing motor car, but examination soon revealed that a dastardly crime had been committed. Constable Gutteridge had been fired at from close range by someone using a heavy revolver of Army pattern. Four shots were fired in all, aimed at the head, which was terribly injured. Not a single definite clue was left behind, but the dead man's colleagues of the Essex Constabulary started in grim earnest to unravel the mystery. Later in the day Scotland Yard experts were called in to co-operate.'

The story began on Monday, 26th September 1927. PC Gutteridge, a popular local policeman, was seen that evening by several people in the Stapleford Abbotts area as he passed on the regular cycle patrols of his beat which he carried on through the night. He was due to meet PC Taylor who worked the adjacent Lambourne End beat at 3.15 on Tuesday morning, about an hour into his regular night shift.

The cartridge case with the distinctive mark which matched it to Browne's gun.

PC George William Gutteridge.

They came together at the appointed time, exchanged news of happenings in the area, then parted again to make their way back along their beats and to a welcome cup of tea at home. PC Taylor was the last-known local person to see George Gutteridge alive. Moving ever further away from him on his cycle, PC Taylor heard nothing in that silent, sleeping countryside to give him the slightest suspicion that his colleague was in the gravest danger.

But on that night two people did hear something which interrupted their sleep. Gertrude, Lady Decies, who was then living at the Beresford Tea Gardens close to the main road at Stapleford Abbotts, heard a motor car, most unusual in those days at that time of night, between half past three and four on the Tuesday morning. It sounded as if it was being driven 'at a terrific speed', as she put it, towards Ongar. A few moments later she heard the bang of a gun being fired. Montague Martin, a farmer asleep within a quarter of a mile of the site of the tragedy said he was woken by the sound of a gun between three and four in the morning, but as he heard no more shots he went back to sleep.

The man most shocked by the shooting was the one who made the grisly discovery. Alec Ward got up early every day to deliver mail from Romford to all the local post offices out to Abridge and back.

By six o'clock on Tuesday morning he was well on his way, just about a mile from Stapleford Tawney post office, his next delivery point. It was still dark as he drove his van down the hill leading to Passingford Bridge, but his headlights caught the bulk and form of something lying in the road. He pulled up and climbed out of the van to investigate. To his shock and horror he saw the body of a policeman in uniform, stretched out on his back, in the middle of a pool of blood. Alec shouted nervously as he approached, 'Is that you, Bill?' for he knew PC Gutteridge from regular greetings exchanged as they passed on the road. There was no reply. He came a little closer, overcoming his revulsion at the sight of the dreadfully injured face with its eyes apparently gouged out. Then he realised that the policeman was quite dead. He was not to know until later that the man had been dead for some three hours. Dead, with his pencil still grasped in his right hand, and his notebook opened to a blank page right beside him, as if he were about to take down some details from another person. His whistle was out of his pocket and his helmet was lying a few feet away, while his cape was thrown back over his shoulders.

Luckily a young lad came cycling along to his work and Alec Ward sent him off at once to get help. The lad rode quickly to the farm at Stapleford Hall, run by his uncle J.R. Saward, and he rushed back with what first aid materials and blankets he could quickly muster. Alec, on a tight delivery schedule, left him there and drove on to Stapleford Tawney, very much shaken. At the post office he telephoned the police at Romford and Havering as well as sending other helpers to the scene. PC Bloxham, from Havering, was the first on the scene, followed by a number of other officers in cars and on cycles. The road was closed until Dr Woodhouse from Romford had time to examine the body. He confirmed that the man had been shot more than once and that the murderer must have used a heavy calibre military weapon to inflict such injuries.

Of course, the police were outraged by this callous killing of one of their colleagues and a determined effort to catch the murderer was immediately put in hand. Scotland Yard was contacted at once and Chief Inspector Berrett and Sergeant Harris of the CID were sent down in the fastest car the Yard had. A very close search of the scene of the crime showed that four shots had been fired. Two bullets hit the policeman when he was standing up – sufficient to have caused his death in seconds; but it appeared that even as he lay dying the brutal murderer fired two more bullets at the closest range – one through each eye. The first two bullets were never found, passing clean through the body they apparently had sped through the roadside hedge and into the field. The second two bullets were found embedded in the road beneath the dead man's head.

One awful circumstance of this crime was that just a quarter of a mile away – two minutes on his bicycle – George Gutteridge's wife was waiting for him at home with his breakfast on the table. A constable had to knock on her door and break the awful news. Lady Decies was one of several neighbours who took it in turns to be with Mrs Gutteridge through this day of grief and desolation. Their children, a girl of twelve and a boy aged four, were looked after by village people until the worst of the shock and grief, the funeral service and the burial were over.

A very important clue came into the detectives' hands more quickly than they could have hoped. They had been told of a car being stolen on that same Tuesday morning at about three o'clock from Dr E.R. Lovell's garage at London Road, Billericay. Local people said they had heard it being driven away. Dr Lovell kept his petrol tank topped up and left his instruments in it overnight so that he could make a quick exit to any emergency in the night. Early on the following day, Wednesday, that car, registration TW 6120, was found abandoned in Foxley Road, Brixton, south-west London, and reported by a sharp-eyed local man. Since Passingford Bridge was just half an hour's run from Dr Lovell's house the police were very interested. They searched the car thoroughly – and found the cartridge case of a bullet which would have been used in an army-issue revolver, similar to the one used in the policeman's murder. What is more, blood stains were detected on the running board by the door on the driver's side. Chief Constable Wensley, one of Scotland Yard's top men, said it could be assumed that this was the very car which PC Gutteridge had stopped on the road. Presumably he had jumped on the running board to prevent it being driven away while he made enquiries, and it was, possibly, a man in the back seat who fired the first two shots.

The paper tells us of the next development: 'Fingerprint experts from Scotland Yard were called to examine the abandoned car. They brought their special fingerprint-powder-blowing apparatus and worked on the car for some hours. They paid special attention to the steering wheel – which they carefully removed from the car for the purpose, and took to Scotland Yard – and the doortops. A large number of fingerprints were found on the car. They were photographed and taken to Scotland Yard, where they were compared with certain other prints in the Criminal Record Office. This comparison resulted in a valuable discovery . . . ' Apparently two sets of prints were those of well-known criminals! The doctor kept a check of the mileage of all his journeys, so he was able to say that since it was stolen the car had travelled 43 miles, and the police found that tallied exactly with a journey from Billericay, over Passingford Bridge, through Abridge and on to the very road in Brixton where it was abandoned. But there the trail went cold. Where were the suspected criminals lying low? Scotland Yard organised a house-to-house search of the Brixton area – all to no avail. For weeks the police were busy as bees, and the media were right behind them. A reward was offered for any information that might lead to an arrest.

Meanwhile life had to go on in Stapleford Abbottts. George Gutteridge had to be decently buried. At what the paper described as an 'Impressive Funeral At Warley', the Bishop of Barking said, 'The whole country has been stirred to its depths by this tragic affair and it is in the deepest sorrow that we join with the mourners in showing our admiration for a brave man and our respect for a force of men to whom we owe so much.' Vast crowds lined the route from the house of PC Gutteridge's brother-in-law in Junction Road, Warley, all the way to Christ Church, waiting quietly, respectfully, as the rain poured down. Two hundred uniformed colleagues, headed by the Chief Constable of Essex, Captain J.A. Unett, marched four abreast in the funeral cortege. They marched in silence; the tramp of feet interspersed only with the sounds of overwhelming grief. The most touching scenes centred on the sorrowing state of the grieving widow and the fatherless daughter. The little boy had been altogether too upset by his mother's grief and sorrow to be present at the funeral. What kind of men would do such a foul deed? The Bishop's closing words are as meaningful now as they were then:

'We would like to think that such a deed would have more likely happened among the wilder tribes who live in other parts of the world. They must be desperadoes – men without hope. It seems so un-English; yet I am afraid it is typical of the spirit that is beginning to find some development among us – a spirit that is not only regardless of property; which is not a small matter, but which thinks nothing of the value of human life, or the affection of human ties which binds a man to those he loves more than life itself.'

The body was laid to rest in Warley cemetery. It took an hour for the procession of mourners to pass by the grave, paying their last respects, and appreciating the banks of flowers which were the only way members of the public could express their deep sorrow, and their gratitude for one policeman's unstinting service.

Police enquiries had taken a new turn. An ex-convict motivated, perhaps, by the rich reward offered by a newspaper, mentioned the name of Frederick Guy Browne, a very vicious criminal who had only just finished a stretch in prison. The 'grass' wrote to the police, saying he had met Browne when they were both serving time in

Dartmoor prison. When he got out he went to see Browne who was renting a garage in Battersea and stealing cars for resale. The 'grass' said that whilst talking to a fellow named Kennedy, the so-called manager of Browne's tacky little business, he noticed a Webley revolver hanging on the office wall and jokingly remarked that he hoped the two of them and that revolver had not been anywhere near Gutteridge. Kennedy replied that, funnily enough, they had been in Essex the day before the murder. Then, when the 'grass' met Browne himself in Sheffield he almost went mad, waved a revolver in the air, said if the 'Bill' ever tried to take him at the garage they would never get out alive, and he would simply disappear in one of the cars he had close at hand. He shouted, 'They're not so fond of pulling up a car at night after what we did to Gutteridge!'

Another man came forward. He was a butcher from Sheffield who, quite innocently, had bought a car from Browne in part-exchange for his own vehicle. Then he discovered, or was told by the police, that his 'new' car had been stolen from a garage in Tooting, London. The police staked out Browne's garage in Battersea, and when he drove in, in the butcher's car, they pounced and took him in for the theft of the motor from Tooting. At the station they searched him, and what do you think they found? Twelve bullets in cartridge cases very

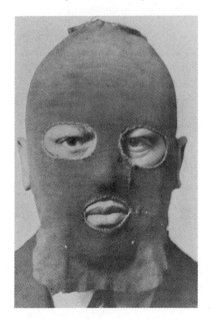

Browne's mask   Chief Inspector Berrett

similar to those found in the road under the murdered policeman. Browne made one very significant remark: 'That's done it. Now it's all up with me.' Then the car itself was searched; a fully-loaded Webley revolver and some of those same 'Mark IV' cartridges were found. 'Ah!' said Browne, 'You've found that, have you; I *am* done for now.' The police then searched his house, in the presence of his wife, and found another revolver. The following day a more intensive search of the car disclosed a gun hidden behind a panel. Later, when interviewed by Chief Inspector Berrett on the charge of car stealing he disclaimed any connection with the Gutteridge murder, but he did confirm that his partner in the car-selling business was William Henry Kennedy.

With Browne still being held on the charge of car stealing the police concentrated on bringing in his partner Kennedy for questioning. He was traced to Liverpool, where he and his wife were renting a room. Detective Sergeant Mattinson, of the Liverpool police, was shadowing him in plain clothes, and was able to get up alongside him, confirm his identification, and say, 'Come on, Bill. Now, then, come on, Bill.' Kennedy swivelled round to face him, pulled out a gun, stuck it in the sergeant's ribs and fired. There was no bang – just a click – he had not taken off the safety catch and the Sergeant was amazed to find himself still alive and upright. His reactions were swift, he grabbed Kennedy's gun hand with his left hand, twisted it up in the air and with his right hand gave Kennedy a hard blow to the head. He wrenched the revolver away from Kennedy, seized him by the collar of his coat, stuck the revolver in his ribs and hustled him up the street, 'shouting at the top of my voice', as he put it. Other officers rushed to his aid and Kennedy was firmly secured. As he was being led away he said to Mattinson, 'I am sorry, I've no grudge against the police, but you should be in heaven now, and there was one for me.' The police found that there truly were just two bullets in the magazine. That was how close these gangsters were to causing the death of a second policeman! This all happened around midnight. By 1.30 am Kennedy had been charged in the matter of stealing the car.

To date Browne's statements had protested complete innocence of implication in George Gutteridge's murder. But now, on 26th January 1928, Chief Inspector Berrett interviewed Kennedy, and told him that he was less interested in the car theft than in the murder. Kennedy replied, 'I may be able to tell you something, but let me consider awhile.' He was allowed to speak to his wife and after 15 minutes he told Berrett that he did not murder George Gutteridge, but he was there when he was shot and he knew who did it. For three hours, from seven to ten o'clock at night he told the whole story.

William Kennedy. Frederick Browne.

It was a complete account of his association with Browne, leading to that fateful day when they boarded the train to Billericay, stole the doctor's car and took all kinds of byways to get to London and the garage unchallenged. '. . . We got on to a kind of main road on the way to Ongar. When we got some distance up on this road we saw some one who stood on the bank and flashed his lamp as a signal to stop. We drove on, and I heard a police whistle, and told Browne to stop. He did so quite willingly, and when the person came up we saw it was a policeman. Browne was driving, and I was sitting on his left in the front. The policeman came up close to the car and stood near Browne and asked him where he was going and where he came from. Browne told him we came from Lea Bridge Garage, and had been out to some repairs. The policeman then asked him if he had a card. Browne said "No." He then asked Browne, "Have you a driving licence?" Browne again said "No." The policeman then again asked him where he had come from, and Browne stammered in his answer, and the policeman then said, "Is the car yours?" I then said, "No; the car is mine." The policeman flashed his light in both our faces and was at this time standing close to the running board on the off-side. He then asked me if I knew the number of the car, and Browne said, "You'll see it on the front of the car." The policeman

91

said, "I know the number, but do you?" I said, "Yes, I can give you the number," and said "TW 6120." He said, "Very well, I'll take particulars," put his torch back in his pocket and pulled out his notebook, and was in the act of writing when I heard a report, quickly followed by another one. I saw the policeman stagger back and fall over by the bank at the hedge. I said to Browne, "What have you done?" and then saw that he had a large Webley revolver in his hand. He said, "Get out quick." I immediately got out and went round to the policeman, who was lying on his back, and Browne came over and said, "I'll finish the bugger," and I said, "For God's sake don't shoot any more, the man's dying," as he was groaning.

'The policeman's eyes were open, and Browne, addressing him, said, "What are you looking at me like that for?" and, stooping down, shot him at close range through both eyes. There were only four shots fired. Browne then said, "Let's get back into the car." We had driven close into the bank, and backed out a little, and drove on in the direction of Ongar. He gave me the revolver, and told me to load it while he drove on. I loaded it and in my excitement dropped an empty shell in the car. The other three I threw away into the roads. We drove at great pace through many villages, the names of which I do not know, but I know we went through Buckhurst Hill, and then Bow and the Elephant and Castle, and while on this journey Browne said, "Have you loaded that gun again? If you have, give it me back." I gave it to him and he put it on the seat by his right-hand side. He wanted to take the car to the garage, but I persuaded him to have nothing to do with the garage. We drove to Brixton, and went up a road I don't know the name of, and drove into a cul-de-sac at about 5.30 am. We left the car and came out into the main road, and came by tramcar back to the garage, bringing with us the two cases out of the car containing doctors' instruments. These, or the majority of them, were smashed up, and the cases were cut up into small pieces, which Browne later took out in his car and distributed about various roads in the country, so as to destroy all evidence, and I did not know that he retained any of the doctor's property.'

Browne threatened to blow out Kennedy's brains if he as much as thought of leaving him. 'You'll stop here and face it out with me!' By 17th December, however, Kennedy stated, Browne allowed Kennedy to go his own way. He went off to West Kirby, Liverpool where he married and returned with his wife on 13th January, 1928. With the enquiries concerning the butcher's stolen car, Kennedy saw that Browne was now a marked man, so he headed back to Liverpool, where he was arrested. The result of his statement was that both men were held in custody for trial at the Central Criminal Court on 23rd April 1928. The police knew it was necessary to find the revolver which fired the bullets at the scene of the crime and here a new, historic step was taken in proving evidence of the use of a particular gun. Sir Wyndham Childs, Assistant Commissioner of the Metropolitan Police, noted the unusual characteristics of the cartridges which expelled the bullets. He was able to show that they had been declared obsolete in the Army in 1914. The black powder they contained had not been in production since 1894. Many a revolver confiscated by the police in the interim had been examined forensically, but none had filled the bill. With Browne's arrest and the finding of his Webley revolver, it was put under microscopic photographic examination. The resultant photographs showed that his gun, the cartridges found upon him and the cartridge lost in the car all bore the marks consistent with their firing in that particular gun – in other words 'gun prints', as certain as fingerprints.

It was a complicated ballistic explanation which had to be given to the 'twelve good men and true'. For five days the jury listened to the evidence. At the end of the judge's summing up they took just two hours and 18 minutes to find both defendants guilty of murder. Appeals made by both men on 22nd May were turned down. On 31st May, Browne and Kennedy were executed at Pentonville and Wandsworth prisons respectively. That last despicable shooting through the eyes can be put down to Browne's mistaken belief in the old superstition that a dead man's eyes retain an image of the last face to have looked into them. Public medical knowledge has since moved on.

11

THE SADDEST STORY OF ALL

THE MURDER OF PAMELA COVENTRY AT HORNCHURCH,
JANUARY 1939

Little Pamela Coventry was just nine years old. She had come home from her school in Benshurst Avenue, Hornchurch, on Wednesday 18th January 1939, to have dinner with her Mum, or stepmother, to be precise. Her Dad was away in Lincolnshire, busy at his work as an electrician. Pamela looked so neat in her green gymslip with its red, fringed girdle and fawn woollen stockings when she got ready for the 15 minute walk back to school. She put on her brown wellington boots, her blue swagger coat with chromium buttons, very posh, cut down from a real grown-up's coat, and a pale green beret. 'Don't forget your dancing shoes,' said her Mum, putting them in a paper bag so she could tuck them under her arm. She liked those slippers, red leather, trimmed with black fur, she felt good in them.

Her parents loved her very much and did their best for her. That included not only the dancing but also music lessons at a house in Diban Avenue. A fortnight previously she had come home at half-past six after a music lesson and asked her Mum as soon as she got in: 'Can I go on an errand for a man who lives in Coronation Drive?' 'Where did you meet this man?' – 'As I was coming home from music' – 'No, I don't want you to do that, you're out late enough after dark as it is.' Pamela would not want to displease her Mum.

Now they cheerily waved to each other as she went off up Morecambe Close into Coronation Drive, from where she would have gone across the bridge over the railway at Elm Park station, into Benshurst Avenue and so into the school itself.

But Pamela never got to school that afternoon. Her Mum went there as usual to meet her and bring her home, but while lots of parents and children passed by her at the gates there was still no sign of her little girl. She asked one or two of Pamela's home-going

94

1940

A traffic motorcyclist seen at Thaxted, 1940 *(Essex Police Museum)*

friends if she had already come out and they told her that Pamela had not been to school at all that afternoon. Mrs Coventry was getting rather worried. Perhaps the naughty girl had gone to a friend's house without telling her. She went round to a number of such friends with no success before she returned home, very tired and now desperately worried, for Pamela was not there. She put on her coat again and went straight to the police station. The police were understanding and sympathetic, but they could not be very helpful in such a situation. They took down the exact description of the little girl as she had set off that lunch-time and said they would keep the sharpest look-out throughout the town.

With her husband away from home Mrs Coventry spent a sleepless, worrying night. No word from the police, no hoped-for knock on the door from Pamela herself, where could she be? Was someone hurting her? Had she run away from home for some reason she could not explain? The questions running through her mind were answered that very next morning.

The scene shifts to Wood Lane, west of Morecambe Close and to a man, Charlie Horseman, riding along it on a bicycle. He was a night-watchman over at Collier Row who had finished work early on Thursday morning, 19th January – but let him tell the story in his own words: 'I had gone on my cycle to see some friends at Hornchurch Aerodrome, where I used to work, but as they were not there I thought I would ride to Chadwell Heath to see my brother. As I turned the corner in Wood Lane, which is rather a deserted spot, surrounded with fields, I could see something lying in a deep ditch a little distance up the lane. I thought it was a parcel, but when I reached the spot I got off my machine and investigated. Looking over the bank I saw it was a naked body, which had apparently been trussed. There was a piece of white material near the neck, but I didn't get into the ditch to see what it was. I immediately went to the RAF house and telephoned to the police.'

You will have gathered that this pathetic, trussed-up bundle was little Pamela Coventry. The police from Romford were over there very quickly, including Superintendent O. Knights and Detective Inspector Baker, along with Inspector Shelley from Upminster. They had the disagreeable task of examining the corpse before they could say that the child had been assaulted, physically and sexually, then strangled and carried to this spot, possibly in a car to be dumped in the ditch. The police now had the unenviable task of breaking the terrible news to Mrs Coventry. But they could not tell her that Pamela was naked, that her legs were drawn up and tied tightly against her chest and her arms bound firmly to her body, using thick black cable, a thinner green cable, pieces of thick string and insulating tape. Before she could be moved to a mortuary for formal identification the Home Office pathologist, Sir Bernard Spilsbury, was called in to make an official forensic examination. Officers from Scotland Yard were called in to assist in the investigation. Meanwhile local police and men from the Royal Air Force stationed at nearby

Hornchurch aerodrome were drafted in to make an extensive search of the locality which, in those days, was largely waste land awaiting development, looking for any signs that the horrific crime had been committed in the general area of the scene of the discovery.

Sir Bernard Spilsbury was able, from his expert examination, to present a scenario of Pamela's last moments. Someone must have lured her into a house within half an hour of her leaving home. A house, because the marks on her body corresponded more with a softer, covered floor than the street or bare earth. She had received a terrible blow on the jaw before she was strangled and had fallen, striking her head on a hard surface which raised a bruise and a bump behind her left ear. In the course of this violent attack she had been 'interfered with' as the discreet language of the day put it in the official report.

A curious detail did not escape the pathologist's eagle eye. When the child's body was straightened with limbs extended a cigarette-end was found squashed between leg and chest which could only have found its way there while the body was actually being trussed up and made ready for disposal. It was a hand-rolled cigarette, using loose tobacco in a cigarette paper. Local enquiries were stepped up to such a scale that 3,000 individual enquiries were made on the estate where Pamela had lived. From her friends it was established that she had not met them as arranged at half-past one by the Elm Park railway bridge. Her mother had seen her entering Coronation Drive as she stood at her door, but no one had seen her at the other end of it.

Though the newspapers published details of Pamela's clothing nobody reported seeing any of it – the murderer had taken good care that none would be found, everybody had coal or coke burning stoves in those days. All clothing, that is, except the petticoat tied round her neck, which had caught the finder's attention on that dark morning. But Pamela's brown wellingtons were not so easily disposed of, they were found in a ditch bordering Abbs Cross Lane, three quarters of a mile from Coronation Drive, in the paper bag in which she had been carrying her slippers. There was one more find. In a newspaper parcel fastened with the same kind of insulating tape found on the body were the enamel badge from the gymslip, the buttons from the coat and a piece of cable similar to that used in the trussing-up. The date of that newspaper was 11th January, an important part of the evidence, as will be revealed.

Now the police were confident that the murderer lived in the locality and that a car was not used, as first thought. The police turned to a close examination of the cable and string used in the tying up of the body. They reckoned these pieces had come from someone's garden – used originally for training up runner beans or supporting other plants with the cable in vertical lengths and the string connecting with them horizontally. After patiently checking to find the manufacturer they found that the black-coloured cable had been out of production for twelve years.

They had details of the two types of cable, with photographs, circulated in the national dailies, referring especially to the 'wear' shown on it from its original use – holding back a door or window, 'earthing' a radio, or something like that. Hundreds of people responded, indicative of their outrage at this sick and vicious crime, but no one could identify the cables and string, or the use to which they had been put. There were still two clues to follow up, one was Pamela's reference to the man who lived in Coronation Drive and the other was that cigarette end.

A house-to-house visit throughout Coronation Drive was planned, based upon a specially prepared questionnaire which ensured that all officers asked the same questions of every occupier as to their movements during those essential hours from 1 pm, as evinced from the medical examination. However, it was not a resident of Coronation Drive who gave valuable information to the police, but Mr Walter Gynn, who delivered milk down the street. He came forward to say that a Mrs Richardson of Coronation Drive had asked him to call her husband, to see that he got up each morning at 5 am when the milkman left the milk on the doorstep – she was going into hospital to have a baby and he just would not get up on his own! Mr Gynn obliged for a week, then Mr Richardson told him not to bother any more because he had changed shifts at work and would not have to be in until 2 pm in future. Gynn knew he worked at Dagenham and could say that he definitely saw him, at 1.15 pm on Wednesday 18th January, leave a café at the corner of Wood Lane and cycle along Southend Road from the direction of Coronation Drive. Richardson nodded his head in recognition as he passed, then at the top of Wood Lane he turned back towards Coronation Drive. When the milkman went up that way later on he saw neither Richardson nor Pamela.

A curious thing, he thought, was that while he was doing his milk round at about 5 am the next morning there was a light on in Richardson's kitchen, though Richardson had said he was not due at work till 2 pm and Mrs Richardson was still in hospital. He remarked on it to his assistant at the time. He knew Richardson cycled to work regularly through Wood Lane and so was familiar with its surroundings. From this statement Chief Inspector Bridger reckoned there was enough information to justify an interview on 26th January with Richardson, who made and signed a statement concerning his activities over the significant period. Summed up, it showed he was a 28-year-old married man with one child and the new-born baby, and had lived in Coronation Drive for a couple of years or so. His wife had returned home with the baby on 22nd January. His sister-in-law, Mrs Gray, had been doing the housework while the older child was being cared for elsewhere. He worked at a Dagenham chemical works, cycling there by Southend Road and Ford Lane. He *used* to go by Wood Lane but he gave that up some nine months before when someone put him onto this easier route. It only took him 15 minutes, the same time as by train, but to be safe he usually left home 25 minutes before the hour he clocked on.

He said he remembered Tuesday 17th January quite well. He had been affected at work by some acid fumes which irritated his eyes and throat, but when he got home at about 11.20 pm he decided it was a good time to paint the kitchen, so he worked on until 3 am before going to bed. Next day, Wednesday the 18th, he spent the morning in the kitchen again until half-past twelve, when his sister-in-law came and prepared his dinner for him. He was not feeling too well, so he went to work on the train, leaving home about 1.20 pm to catch the 1.48 or the 1.52 from Elm Park station. When he got there he heard that his opposite number on the early shift had gone home because he too was suffering from those same acid fumes.

At this point Richardson said he had got mixed up – that had happened on Monday, 16th January, not Tuesday. Now he could not remember how he went to work on Tuesday; Monday was by bike, Wednesday was by train. So, on this day, Wednesday, he saw the works manager about the effect of the fumes and was sent home where he arrived about 3 pm. His sister called ten minutes later to pick up her umbrella. He went to bed then and stayed there till around 5.30 pm. Then he cycled up to Elm Park Broadway to buy some putty. After tea he went to the doctor because his eyes were still smarting and got a prescription for conjunctivitis. The chemist told him it would be ready next morning. He went to pick it up about 8 am then got on with the decorating through the day, going to bed around midnight and waking up at nine next morning.

In reply to the Inspector's question he said that during the first week his wife was in hospital he did ask a little girl who was passing the house to go and get him some tobacco, but she ran off. He could not describe her because the light was failing. The incoherent, self-contradictory statement rambled to a close without producing any more useful information. He did not mention seeing the milkman in Wood Lane, nor did he explain why the light in his kitchen was still on, as noticed by the milkman.

While he was busy with the complications of the statement he was told he could smoke if he wanted to, so he produced pouch and cigarette papers and rolled himself a cigarette. Before he finished it the Inspector took it from him, stubbed it out and put it in a test tube. Then he was told to hand over the pouch and the papers. In the pouch were found 14 more stub-ends from cigarettes he had smoked and another was found in a pocket in his jerkin.

The essential facts stated by Richardson were corroborated by the various people involved. The doctor, who had examined him on the 18th said the man's condition was associated more with general shock and nervousness than with his story of being gassed by acid fumes, for his examination found no trace of such gassing.

The police decided it was time to get a warrant to search Richardson's house. Even the vacuum cleaner was brought into use to get samples of dust and fibres for microscopic examination. They found, in a cupboard, a pile of copies of the *News Chronicle*, put away as day followed day, from 6th to 21st January, all were there except for the issue for 11th January. Pamela's badge and coat buttons had been wrapped up in a copy of the *News Chronicle* – dated 11th January! That parcel also included an odd piece of black cable. None was found in the house, but from the garden fence the searchers took samples of tarred string.

Looking at the situation of the house in relation to the place where the body was found the police noted that from Richardson's shed in the back garden it was possible to walk straight across the plots where houses were partly built and come to a field which bordered on Wood Lane, and the path across that field was hidden from view by a hedge. The police paced the route – it took just 450 footsteps to reach the ditch where the body had lain!

On 1st February Richardson's neighbour handed in to the police a length of green cable to which was tied a piece of tarry string. It was given him by Richardson to lengthen the lead of his wireless set. It matched the wire round the body. Mr Curley added that Richardson had told him at 6 pm on 18th January that he was going to the doctor, and he called in again at 8 pm looking 'ill and worried'. Once, around Christmas time, Richardson had confided in him that some of the chemicals he handled, and the fumes engendered, made him feel sexually interested.

The police waited no longer. At 10.45 pm they went to the chemical works and arrested Richardson, took him to the station and charged him with Pamela Coventry's murder. A hastily arranged special court assigned him to police custody for a week.

In the interim Pamela Coventry had been buried on 26th January at Barking cemetery. The *Essex Weekly News* described the public feeling: 'The streets near the house in Morecambe Close, Elm Park, where the little girl lived, were lined with about 2,000 people, who watched the cortege as it proceeded towards Barking, where the Coventrys had formerly lived. The crowds at the cemetery were among the largest seen there, and many women were obviously greatly affected. Three of the relatives, two women and a man, collapsed at the graveside and had to be assisted away by police. Mr and Mrs Coventry, the girl's father and stepmother, and Mrs Coventry, sen., her grandmother, showed signs of distress. The vicar said, "Words fail to express our feelings of horror and shame that such a deed should be done in our land. We express as well as words can express our sympathy to the loved ones of this child, and we pray that the day may not be far distant when such things cannot be done in this land we cherish." ' At that time the paper had said, '... police are still without a clue'. Now they had a suspect.

On 3rd February Leonard Richardson was brought before a special sitting of the Romford Bench, charged with the girl's murder. The evidence was put forward – the cable, the string, the missing newspaper. Richardson was remanded until 10th March, remanded again on that date and finally committed for trial at the Central Criminal Court on 27th March 1939. He pleaded not guilty. Once again all the evidence was put to the court, but strangely it all came to nought. The defending counsel put it to the judge that there was insufficient evidence to prove conclusively that Richardson was the murderer. It should be remembered that the man had never at any time admitted his implication in the slightest degree. The judge appeared to agree with the defence, saying that he could not stop the case now being considered by the jury, but they had the power to stop it if they so wished. He adjourned the court at that point and, after lunch, the foreman of the jury passed a note to the judge that they felt the evidence was not strong enough to convince them, so there and then they gave their verdict of not guilty and Richardson went free.

There had been witnesses who, like one neighbour, said Richardson was 'a jolly good sort' and his wife who said he was 'a jolly good husband'. But the strange thing about the trial was that, as they were all ushered out of a side entrance to escape public attention, the members of the jury stepped forward one by one to shake Richardson by the hand and wish him the best of luck. The foreman, a little pompously, added, 'As foreman of the jury let me congratulate you. All the best, Richardson.' He shook his hand. If that was not the hand which tied the cable and the string, which wrapped the buttons in the newspaper, then who did murder that innocent little girl? The police, who had worked so hard, had no other avenues to explore, and the mystery remains unsolved.

12

THE BOMB IN THE BATH CHAIR

THE MURDER OF ARCHIBALD BROWN AT RAYLEIGH,
JULY 1943

Murderers are not always callous, vicious criminals; there can be the most heart-breaking family circumstances which lead to the final, awful act.

Archibald Brown was a miller, running the family business of T.J. Brown and Son at Rayleigh flour mills on London Hill. He was born in 1896 and in 1920 had a very bad motorcycle accident which may have triggered the progressive disease which by 1940 had rendered him almost helpless in a wheelchair. His wife had already been told that his mental state was deteriorating at the same time. She had for years carried a heavy burden in the constant care for him, while the husband she had known faded away in mind and body. In the process Archibald often became irritable and irrational. Once when his wife was feeding him he tore at her clothes; at other times in frustrated rage he had hit out and scratched her arm, once he had even tried to get his hands round her throat. In his condition these outbreaks of violence were not life-threatening, but they were frightening. In the latter days Mrs Brown was able to afford the services of a trained nurse to bear the brunt of her husband's care.

They had two sons, Eric James, born in 1923, and Colin, three years his junior. Though in his childhood days Eric always seemed to rub his father up the wrong way they did become much closer as he reached his late teens. There were some members of the wider family, going back three generations, who were known to have been mentally unstable; one had committed suicide. With this background it is not surprising to hear that acquaintances at school and at work averred that Eric was a rather strange lad. In his first job, as a trainee bank clerk, his behaviour was often so odd that in the end he was asked to hand in his resignation, or be dismissed. He had what the manager called 'brainstorms' during which he would wave his fists in the air and then thump them down on the desk.

Eric found a complete change of occupation, out in the open fields where he helped his uncle Frederick Brown on his poultry farm off Lark Hill Road, Canewdon, until he was called up for military service. On 1st October 1942, in the middle of the Second World War, he became a private in the 8th Battalion, the Suffolk Regiment. Mrs Brown was extremely attached to her eldest son and felt very protective of him. She wrote to his Commanding Officer at the beginning of June 1943 and asked if he would grant Eric compassionate leave because of the serious illness of his father, and it was granted. While on leave he helped in the mill next to the house.

In conversation with his mother of an evening he told her he noticed that his father had really gone downhill. He was so rude and rough to her that Eric wondered how she put up with it. Only when the sad story was all over did Mrs Brown tell the police of the true situation at home, as recorded by Superintendent G.H. Totterdell in his autobiography: 'Eric, she said, was about three and a half years old when Colin, the younger brother, was born. From the outset the husband had favoured the younger boy, which had amounted to positive dislike of the older lad. When Eric had been at Rayleigh Grammar School his home-life by reason of his father's persecution had been miserable. At meal-times Mrs Brown had feared to let him sit close to his father. At the slightest noise when he was eating his father would strike the boy across the head. On one occasion he had struck him across the face for no reason at all. There were other senseless and inordinate punishments: the writing of the line, "I must not make a noise", five hundred times, with every ten lines marked off, the more easily to be corrected – which had taken the little boy all evening, and ended in tears, while Colin was out playing; the running from office door to front door down the whole length of the hall a hundred times, till the child was exhausted; the solitary confinement in a dark cupboard under the stairs or in the store-shed. And all for the merest unintentional mistake on the boy's part.' Small wonder then that a simmering resentment had stayed with Eric into his manhood.

Now Eric had become very conscious of just what his mother was having to endure. He decided that he would have to do something and had been thinking about it more while he was in the army. Perhaps it was his sudden transfer from his home comforts, his caring mother and his quiet life that triggered something in his brain. It gave him an idea, with no real planning or determination. He looked round the army camp for some means to these vague ends. Part of his army training had been in the use of the Hawkins 75 grenade

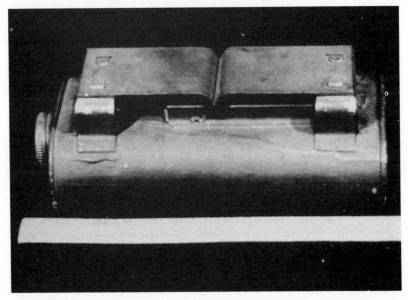

A Hawkins No 75 grenade mine of the type hidden in the bathchair.

mine. Here in the Spilbury depot there were at least 200 of these mines; 50 or so were kept for training and familiarisation and there were also instructional pamphlets available. For a man who only wanted one mine, a man who had worked in the orderly room and knew the movements of people in charge, it was not so difficult to appropriate this.

When he came home on compassionate leave that last time he brought with him, in an attache case, a Hawkins 75 mine under a bundle of dirty washing. He had plenty of time, while his mother and the nurse were busy with his father, to slip round to the air raid shelter in the garden and to hide the mine in the big tool box there. Putting the case with the dirty linen back in his bedroom, he waited for his mother to ask him if he had any laundry. When she did he gave her the key to the case for her to unlock herself – a perfectly innocent case of dirty clothes! For the next fortnight he deliberated as to what he should do with that mine – if anything at all, for it would be the final step – no going back. The resolve grew stronger in his mind that he must deliver his father from his mental and physical suffering and bring to his mother release at last from the torment of waiting upon her husband at every tinkle of his bell, day and night; to bring peace at last to this troubled family.

After lunch on 23rd July he slipped round to the air raid shelter, in which his father's invalid chair was kept. He bolted the door against surprise and got the mine out of the tool box. He primed it so that it would be set off by what he judged would be the weight of his father's body and placed it, completely hidden, under the brown velveteen cushion of the seat, between it and the canvas bottom. The deed was done, but what a fright he had; even as he was adjusting it someone tried to open the door. It was Nurse Mitchell, come to collect the chair to take Mr Brown for his usual fresh-air excursion towards Hockley and back.

The nurse rattled that door no end before going off, grumbling to herself, to tell Mrs Brown she could not open it. When the two of them came back to try again they saw Eric in the very act of opening that door. They asked him what on earth he was doing in there that he needed to lock the door, but Eric just prevaricated and made himself scarce. The two of them took the chair round to the house and helped Mr Brown into it, in his pyjamas and dressing gown. He sat down heavily – nothing happened! They fussed over him with blanket, rug and pillows, tucking the ends in neatly under the seat cushion. Then, saying goodbye to Mrs Brown, Nurse Mitchell set off with her patient. They had covered a good mile down the Hockley road when Mr Brown began to fumble at his dressing gown pocket. Nurse Mitchell knew that he was after a cigarette, but that he would not make it on his own. She stopped, went round the chair to face him, got his cigarette case out, put a cigarette between his lips, and lit it for him. It was a pleasant afternoon but soon, she thought, it would be time to turn back.

She grasped the handles of the chair and pushed off again, while Mr Brown shifted a little to make himself comfortable. At that moment there was a mighty explosion. Nurse Mitchell knew nothing of it, the blast had knocked her unconscious to the ground. It must have been Mr Brown's last wriggle for extra comfort which set off the mine's mechanism. He could have known nothing of pain and suffering for his body was torn apart in that split second.

Nurse Mitchell recalled regaining consciousness and seeing her patient's head and shoulders in the road before her. One leg was caught up in a tree and the other was found 16 yards away in someone's front garden. The shock of it stunned everybody in the area for a moment, they thought an enemy plane had dropped a bomb and were waiting for the rest of the salvo. Elsie Mitchell told the court later: 'Suddenly there was a terrific bang. I could smell my hair burning, and a terrific heat came up from somewhere. I saw the head and shoulders of my patient in front, and I think I saw a leg in a tree. My own legs were pumping blood badly. Small pieces of metal were embedded in them. I received treatment in a house, and was

The bathchair after the explosion.

admitted to hospital.' Then came the police to organise help for the nurse and other badly shocked people, to redirect traffic and to gather up the grisly remains of that broken body and the shattered wheelchair.

Superintendent Totterdell was put in charge of inquiries. He first interviewed Mrs Brown and gained a fair idea of the situation in the miller's home. It became quite clear to him that she did not have the knowledge or the means to cause such an explosion, but it was brought out that her soldier son Eric was interested in things mechanical and could even mend the wireless when it went wrong. This was a useful straw in the wind. From the debris Totterdell could see that the explosion had been caused by a mine of some sort. He had a mine of similar type and shape fixed into an identical wheelchair and found that it could lie there undetected by sitters or pushers, but they never did find out how Eric Brown's mine was not set off by Mr Brown's weight when he was first lowered by the ladies into the chair. Totterdell could only hazard the hypothesis that ' . . . it was not until Brown had shifted his weight after Nurse Mitchell had lit his cigarette and moved forward with the chair that readjustment of the dead man's body had set the mechanism in motion.' The Superintendent interviewed Eric Brown next day. After some hesitation he made a complete confession, closing with the words, 'My father is now out of his suffering and I earnestly hope that my mother will now live a much happier and normal life.' His formal arrest followed. On appearance at the Southend County Petty Sessions on 12th September he was held in custody to await trial at the Chelmsford Assizes on 4th November 1943.

It was not a long hearing. The defence was that Brown was insane at the time he placed the mine under the chair. The mangled wreck of that chair was exhibited in court. The paper described the accused as ' . . . a dark-haired, pale-faced young fellow in a neat blue suit, with an open-necked white shirt. His hands were clasped behind his back. There his interest in the proceedings appeared to terminate'. He remained indifferent to his surroundings throughout the trial. His statement, a total confession in fact, was read out by the counsel for the prosecution.

Then Detective Inspector Barkway testified that there had been insanity in the family. He was followed by a neurologist, Dr Hill, who had examined Brown in prison after he had made a token attempt at suicide by slashing his throat. The doctor said that in his opinion Brown was schizophrenic, chronically shy and living in a fantasy world. If Brown had had no one to take care of him the doctor thought that the man would before now have been certifiable as insane. Brown had told him that for the first few weeks in prison he had had such a buoyant feeling, until he suddenly realised that people might call him a murderer.

The jury took just 45 minutes to decide that Brown was guilty but insane. Mr Justice Atkinson used the usual phrase in ordering that he 'be detained during His Majesty's pleasure'.

13

THE CORPSE FROM THE SEA

THE MURDER OF STANLEY SETTY,
OCTOBER 1949

Even murders have their own grisly records. In this case a headless corpse was thrown into the sea, but the crudely fashioned parcel floated and was washed ashore. It was the first time ever in Britain that a body was dropped from the air over the sea in an attempt to dispose of it.

The victim was Stanley Setty. His demise made no great impact on the world at large or even on the world in which he had made his living, the shady car-dealing which, after the war, had evolved in London's Warren Street and its neighbourhood. Dealers paraded their cars in the street and bargained on the pavement with clients who paid cash down and no questions asked. Setty certainly did not deserve to die. He had enjoyed a good run for his money in that he had been dealing in cars, in one way or another, for 25 years in the London area. He had been born in Iraq, it is said to a lady of that country and a Manchester man working over there for an English textiles firm.

Stanley Setty disappeared on 4th October 1949. At 3.30 pm on that day he telephoned his fiancée, Constance Palfreyman to say that he would not be able to see her next day because he had to go to Watford to clinch a deal. Driving towards Euston Road later that afternoon he saw his sister, Mrs Eva Ouri, at whose house he was then living. He stopped to tell her he would not be home for dinner that night. The last person, apart from his killer, to see him alive was a business acquaintance, as he was driving along Great Portland Street at 5.50 pm. He had a passenger who was not recognized.

When he had not arrived home by midnight his sister began to worry. A man in the secondhand car business in the competitive, not to say vicious environment of Warren Street dealt with many a doubtful character. Quick deals on the pavement meant that a man could carry hundreds of pounds on him during the day. 'Dodgy' cars sold to the wrong people could bring swift retribution. Or Setty could have had an accident in one of his cars any hour of the day. His brother-in-law rang the police. They had no record of such an accident, nor did the hospitals. When he had not come home by nine on the following morning checks were made on his last recorded actions. They showed that he had on him at the end of the previous day no less than £1,055, all in £5 notes. This was a considerable sum

What Sidney Tiffen found – a headless, legless torso *(Essex Chronicle)*

at that time. Had someone been tempted to relieve him of it? His car was found abandoned in Chester Place, St Pancras. All the routines in such a case were followed through by the police, but not a clue was found as to Setty's whereabouts or to the state of his health. His sister quickly offered a reward of £1,000 for his discovery. There was total silence.

It stayed that way until 21st October, when the scene shifts to rural Essex, to Tillingham where the tide creeps in twice a day over the marshes and saltings which stretch out miles from the sea wall. Sidney Tiffen was out there in his punt, looking to bag a few wild fowl to supplement his wages of an agricultural labourer. Paddling his punt to creep up on the birds he saw a big parcel, about three feet square which had floated in on the tide. Was this his lucky day? A few bottles of smuggled gin or some other contraband? The coast was famous for it. A difficult job cutting the string in that wobbly punt, but he did it, pulled the wrappings apart, and saw to his horror that it was half of a man's body! The arms were there, tied firmly behind the back, but there was no head, and the legs had obviously been cut off.

Tiffen was not too surprised because this was the ninth corpse he had come across in a long life of wildfowling. He took a look at the body, close enough to see that there were signs of a stab wound in the area of the heart. Knowing the ways of the sea, he had a stake with him which he drove down into the mud and to which he tied the parcel. Thus he prevented it from drifting out again on the next tide and the stake was a good marker for finding the spot again. He headed for the sea wall, then contacted the police at Bradwell-on-Sea. Two constables were sent down to Tillingham and Tiffen guided them at low tide across the marshes to the gruesome remains.

They were bagged and taken quickly to the mortuary at St John's Hospital at Chelmsford. By 1.30 pm the pathologist, Dr Camps, had been informed and was on his way to make a post-mortem examination. He confirmed that stab wounds in the chest caused the man's death. The severing of the head and legs, using a very sharp knife and a saw obviously had resulted in a great outpouring of blood. The trousers had been cut through at the same point as the legs, the remains still attached by braces to the body. The senior police officer present, hearing the pathologist's comments, replied that he thought this could be Stanley Setty's body and asked for a specimen of skin for fingerprints. Dr Camps simply snicked the skin round both wrists and, peeling it off like a pair of rubber gloves, popped it into a container for its journey to Scotland Yard where the records showed that the officer was right – Stanley Setty had been found.

The Auster G-AGXT hired by Hume.

It must be remembered that the police then had no knowledge that an aeroplane had been used in the disposal of the corpse. They had to start patiently with blanket searches of the area where the parcel came ashore for the rest of the body. The press had the story almost at once, the *Times* publishing the discovery on 24th October, just two days after the identification. Just for once this was of great advantage to the police in their enquiries for, having seen the papers, a director of the United Services Flying Club at Elstree called them to say that he might have some useful information. John Simpson, who was also the club's chief engineer, said that a member of the club had acted, he thought, rather suspiciously.

On 5th October this member, Brian Douglas Hume, had hired one of the club's planes, the Auster G-AGXT. He took off around 5 pm heading, he said, for Southend in Essex. At mid-morning next day he appeared again at Elstree, in a car, saying he had left the Auster at Southend Airport and was going down there straight away to bring it back. The next message Elstree received was from Gravesend Aerodrome; the Auster had landed there at 5.45 pm with the weather closing in. Mr Simpson then sent a pilot to bring it back. They looked it over and found the window on the right-hand side had been damaged and the sliding panel ahead of it had been so jammed back that it had to be freed mechanically.

This odd incident led to a close police enquiry at Elstree. An aircraft mechanic stated that around that same date, 5th October, he saw Hume take a parcel from his car and put it into the Auster. William Davy, aircraft fitter, was even more definite. He saw Hume at 5 pm on 5th October, take two parcels from a motor car and put one in the co-pilot's seat and the other just behind it. Both parcels he described as 'bulky'. The question the police now wanted answered was, were those parcels there when the Auster landed at Southend? It was a coincidence that James Small, a member of the Elstree club, was staying at the Southend club on 5th October and saw Hume land in the Auster. He went up to it but saw no parcels inside. The manager of Southend Airport also confirmed that the Auster had landed then. Owen Rawlings, a taxi-driver at Southend Airport said the pilot of G-AGXT hired his taxi to Golders Green on 5th October and paid him with a £5 note from a whole roll of them he brought from his pocket.

On 6th October Hume was back at Southend. At 4 pm he was seen carrying 'a large and heavy package' from his car to the Auster, curtly refusing offers of help. He said he was heading for Elstree with that parcel, but landed at Gravesend. Nobody saw him with a parcel there, and he was very quickly away again in a taxi back to Golders Green to his flat at 623 Finchley Road.

The *Essex Chronicle* of 29th October summed up the situation at that time: '... so unflagging is the search that if I were the murderer I should by now be trembling in my shoes ... Here is the heart of the riddle. Setty was a man of 44. His killers cut off his head and legs, leaving about two inches of each thigh. Was it carelessness on their part which led them to leave the hands? It was by fingerprints that the corpse was identified. Here we can only conjecture. To offer an individual opinion, one might suggest that the body was cut up in that way to make a convenient parcel. The torso was heavy enough as it was. So say men who lifted it. It would not be easy to carry any distance. One simply could not believe that the murderers staggered about on the marshlands off the Essex coast with a torso weighing ten or eleven stone. Certainly a modern way of disposing of such an awkward burden would be to drop it into the North Sea from an aircraft. But you have got to put it into the aircraft first. There are plenty of people on any busy airport who have time to notice anything queer going on ... The needle is in the haystack, but to find it is a rare business. The police have already interviewed scores of people, many in Southend, who were acquainted with Setty ... Chelmsford came very much into the picture at one time in connection with the travels of a certain motor car. Furthermore, it had the distinction of being the headquarters of the Scotland Yard man in charge of the case, Supt Colin MacDougal.

'Supt MacDougal stayed at the Saracen's Head in Chelmsford for three nights at the beginning of the week, leaving on Wednesday for London. He is a quiet man in the middle forties, dressed in a blue pin-stripe suit. Over this he wore a dark overcoat. Every morning, after a punctual 8 am breakfast, a police car from Essex Headquarters called for him. Most nights he did not return till after midnight.' Surely this account demonstrates the determination of the police to 'get a result' as they might put it.

Their next step was an interview with Hume. Apart from one moment when he put his head in his hands and said, 'I'm several kinds of a bastard, aren't I?' he maintained a calm and collected attitude and willingly made a statement. It included the fact that he did know two motor dealers in Warren Street, neither of whom was Setty. He went on to tell a story of meeting men without surnames who were willing to pay for his services, for he was known in the underworld as 'the flying smuggler'. 'Mac', fair-haired, heavily built, 'Gree', a Cypriot, and 'Boy', wanted him to dispose of three parcels and offered him a lot of money. He took the parcels in the Auster and threw them out as they requested. They had told him that they contained the plates and the presses used to manufacture forged petrol coupons. So what the witnesses had seen was exactly what he was doing, and that was why secrecy was vital. One of the parcels had to be kept in his flat overnight. It was so heavy that he had to have some help from the chauffeur of the car he had hired. Once it was in the car he dispensed with the chauffeur's services and set off on his own to Southend. As to the large amount of money people had seen him flashing about, well, it was what he got from the gang for his services!

It was only on 7th October that he thought to check the numbers of the £5 notes against those shown by the newspapers as having been in Setty's possession. He then got rid of as many of them as he could in his wife and child's savings accounts and through his wife's usual expenditure at shops in her housekeeping. He declared he did have a warning call from the gang about keeping his mouth shut and, after that, not another word – and no addresses or other details, of course. The police followed up these vague names and descriptions, through their criminal records, the underworld 'grapevine' and public appeals in the press. Nobody had ever heard of them. But the police had found out that on 5th October Hume took a knife to his local garage to be sharpened. They felt they had enough circumstantial evidence to charge him on 29th October in the Bow Street Magistrates Court where they were successful in having him remanded in custody on a charge of murder.

Now they were able to get a warrant to search his house very carefully. On that same day they found the lounge carpet had a big blood stain on it, but it had recently been cleaned so thoroughly that it would not reveal the blood group. Hume claimed it was simply drink spilt at a party. Then the Director of the Metropolitan Police

Laboratory, Dr Holden, went back to the flat two days later and took up some floorboards in the living room. Enough blood had been spilt there to drip down and soak into the lath and plaster of the ceiling below. A third visit on 1st November discovered blood on the edge of the linoleum in the hall, on the walls up the stairs to the bathroom and on the stairs themselves. To the layman the evidence would seem incontrovertible.

On 18th January 1950 Brian Douglas Hume, aged 29, was brought to trial for murder at the Central Criminal Court, defended by Mr R.F. Levy and Mr Claud Duveen. Mr Christian Humphreys, counsel for the prosecution, opened the trial by admitting that the case was 'almost entirely circumstantial'. The prosecutor could call nobody to say that they actually saw Hume murder Setty: and he had not confessed to it. Mr Humphreys alleged that Hume *did* know Setty through the Warren Street car-dealing fraternity. It could be proved that Hume was very hard up on 4th October while Setty had £1,000 in his pocket. He disappeared that night, and a couple of days later Hume was stripping fivers off a bankroll to pay for taxis from Kent. It seems clear that Setty's body was cut up in Hume's flat. Hume had said he wanted the knife sharpened to carve a joint, but the lady who worked for him was ready to declare on oath that there was no joint of meat in the flat at that time. Hume had also told her on 5th October that he had been washing a carpet. Witnesses as to his movements at various airports told their story and the day ended with the jury being taken by coach to see the flat.

The second day, 19th January, was a bit of an anticlimax. The judge had been taken ill suddenly, so Mr Justice Sellers had to take his place. The jury had to be re-sworn and the witnesses had to give their evidence again, albeit very briefly. There was a long interlude after the defence informed the judge that a national newspaper had tried to persuade a witness not to give evidence and its representative was thoroughly dressed down by the judge. On the third day Hume disarmed the prosecution by admitting to all his actions with the aeroplane and the parcels which he undertook solely on behalf of the mysterious gang of three and simply for the money he received. He only saw the blood in his flat after he had disposed of the third parcel, so he cleaned it up and had the floor restained. He happily admitted that he was quite prepared, for money, to help people evade the charge of forging petrol coupons, 'I am a semi-honest man, but I am not a murderer'.

On Thursday 26th January, the judge finished his summing up. The jury went out at 12.30 pm, returned at 3 pm and the foreman told the judge they could not agree and doubted if they ever would be able to declare a unanimous decision. They were discharged, the prosecution offered no evidence against Hume to the new jury and they were directed by the judge to return a verdict of not guilty.

Then Hume was charged with 'being an accessory after the fact to murder, knowing that a certain person or persons unknown on October 4th, 1949 murdered Stanley Setty, you, on October 5th or 6th 1949, assisted and maintained those person or persons by disposing of the body of the said Stanley Setty'. To this charge Hume did plead guilty. He could have been sentenced to life imprisonment, but he was let off lightly with a sentence of just twelve years.

Warren Street, Setty, Hume – the tide of outrageous modern crimes has washed away their memory.

14

A CASE OF MISTAKEN IDENTITY

THE MURDER OF MURIEL PATIENCE AT BRAINTREE,
NOVEMBER 1972

Braintree is still a quiet country town. The traffic roars round it, shoppers saunter through it, the main square is still given over to the weekly market. Until 1972 its claim to fame was as the home of the great Courtauld textile company founded in 1825 by Samuel Courtauld. Its new-found notoriety was blazed in newspapers throughout the land as THE BARN MURDER. It started like this:

In 1962 Bob Patience and his wife Muriel had come to the Barn Restaurant, on the Rayne Road west of Braintree, building up the business from modest tearooms to a night-spot which drew people from as far away as London, including clientele – among them not a few well-breeched criminals – from their former club, the Ranch House in Ilford.

After a successful night at the Barn, when over 350 guests had wined, dined and danced, by the early hours of the morning of 5th November 1972 there were still plenty of people dancing to the band. Leaving his son David with these revellers, Bob Patience ferried home members of staff who had completed their shift, while Muriel and their daughter Beverley returned to their home, just across the car park. They had left the hall and porch lights on; as they opened the front door there was nothing to warn them of the horror to come.

Beverley entered first and went on through to the kitchen with meat for the dog. Almost before she switched on the light she saw them standing in the shadows – two men, one holding a gun. She tried to push her mother back, but too late – the men were upon her, ordering them to go into the lounge and sit down.

Meanwhile Bob Patience had done the chauffeuring of his staff and about 2.15 am was walking round the property, including the new

116

Left to right: son David, Muriel Patience, Bob Patience and daughter Beverley.

The Patiences' house – opposite the Barn.

motel he had recently opened. He dropped into the house as he passed and walked into the lounge to be confronted by the robber holding the gun, now nestling in a pink cushion as a crude but effective silencer. Muriel had calmed down as the situation developed. 'Don't do anything Bob, they've got a gun,' she cried urgently. Bob sat down near his wife and daughter. Then with the gun pointing threateningly the man asked Bob for the key to the safe which he and his companion had already 'sussed out' in the hall. Bob stalled for time. He had a key in that very room, but he said it was in the restaurant and anyway, the safe was empty. As the music of the late-night revellers drifted over he said, 'You can hear the music; there are cabaret artists over there who have to be paid, and I always pay them; so in a very short time somebody will come looking for me. If you promise not to harm my wife and daughter I'll take you over there and we can get the keys.' Impasse. The gunman repeated his demand for the key several times, Bob reiterated his offer. Finally the man pointed the cushioned gun at the women and threatened, 'Your wife or your daughter?' Then, quite slowly, 'Your wife I think', and pulled the trigger. There was a muffled explosion, the bullet penetrated Muriel's right temple and she gave one scream then slumped over. Bob shouted, 'You've murdered my wife!' He had played a game of bluff – and had lost. Going over to the mantelpiece he took the keys from a bowl.

With the gunman and his companion behind him he walked to the safe in the hall and opened it. He took out £2,000 in cheques and credit card slips, and £400 in cash. The robbers did not know that he had left £7,300 in cash in a secret compartment, or that he deftly avoided delivering up his wife's jewellery, left there in an anonymous cloth bag.

Muriel, poor woman, had been left unattended save for a towel wrapped round her head to staunch the blood by the second intruder who now, after helping the gunman to bind and gag Bob and Beverley, left the house, presumably to arrange a getaway car. When he had gone the gunman, again using the cushion as silencer, cold-bloodedly shot Bob and Beverley, determined that there should be no witnesses to identify them. But Bob came round a few minutes after the robbers had taken his son David's car and fled.

Though bound and gagged Bob was able to summon help by rolling across the floor to the intercom system between house and restaurant and punching all the buttons. David, working in the restaurant without the slightest inkling of the tragedy being played out in the house, recognised his father's gagged cries on the intercom and dashed over as the robbers roared past him in his own car. Within 15 minutes of the 999 call David made at 2.32 am on Saturday

5th November the police arrived at the Barn, where they found all three members of the Patience family still awaiting an ambulance. 'For God's sake get them to hospital,' shouted Bob, pointing to his wife and daughter. The bullet had lodged in Muriel's brain, part of which was now oozing through the wound. As she was being laid on a stretcher by the ambulance men a cartridge case fell out of her clothing. This was vital evidence. A policeman picked it up along with another he had found nearby. As Beverley was being transferred from the ambulance to the hospital the bullet which had passed through her body fell out of her clothes. Bob received treatment for his head injury at Oldchurch Hospital, Romford. Beverley, who took a long time to recover consciousness, was soon in the hands of the experts at Black Notley. Her mother had to be transferred to the special care unit at Oldchurch Hospital but within three days she was dead. It was now a murder enquiry.

The police were at a loss. It seemed that Bob had not been able to identify assailants who apparently knew him well. Beverley, however, was able to describe them. One was blond, early thirties, slim, about five feet eight, short, receding very sandy hair. Intense blue eyes, white even teeth and sallow complexion. He had a slight, Yorkshire accent. When, with surprising calm, Muriel had asked, 'Where do you come from, Yorkshire?' he just grinned and said, 'Not far off'. The other man was about 27, tall, over six feet, broad-shouldered, slim waisted, dark brown hair, brown eyes, wearing a light, grey tweed suit and a tartan-coloured scarf. Not bad descriptions when you know that at the time she spoke Beverley was lying in Black Notley Hospital having undergone an emergency operation to stem the awful damage to her back, liver and stomach by the bullet which passed straight through her body.

Meanwhile the robbers had got clean away in David's car, heading for Dunmow on the A120. We now know their names were Nicholas de Clare Johnson and John Brook. Johnson's experience in car-stealing told him that police would already be alerted over a wide area, so they abandoned the car after a few hectic miles and threw pursuers off the scent by taking to the fields. At about three o'clock in the morning they came to a line of the disused railway track that ran on to Dunmow. The pouring rain made for a miserable, exhausting journey. On the way Johnson asked about the shots he had heard while he was fetching the car. 'There are no witnesses now,' Brook replied, 'I shot the girl through her back to her heart and the man had one in the head.' He was not to know that the bullet which damaged Bob's ear literally bounced off his skull, saving his life. Johnson was very angry that he had been drawn into a murder rap, but Brook laughed in the rain, 'You want to be careful, I've still got the gun!'

A newspaper photograph of
Nicholas de Clare Johnson.

John Brook, the convicted
murderer.

Dawn was glimmering when the bedraggled pair saw a pillbox gun emplacement left over from the last war. It represented shelter from the appalling weather and a chance to draw breath. There they shared the money, burnt and buried the ashes of the bags, cheques and credit slips and found themselves each the richer by just £200, at the cost of death and serious injury to their victims.

Arriving at a road they hitch-hiked to Chelmsford, bought train tickets to London and disappeared into the anonymous crowd where they split up. Johnson was, in fact, on parole from Pentonville prior to completing a sentence already imposed upon him for petty crime. The murder had preyed on his mind. As soon as he could, he put his share of the money in a dustbin, and burnt it. He had told the prison governor that he would be at Romsey over the weekend, so he went there to spend the day with a friend and returned to prison on time that night, staying there until his release in January 1973. Brook had lodgings in London and returned there to get smartened up before going on to Leeds to spend a week with his grandmother.

On the Sunday after the murder the police incident room was in operation. There they obtained the old files dealing with the incident outside Bob's 'Ranch House' back in 1961 which had led to the family being given police protection over two months. Their house here at Braintree had been broken into before, by local youths in 1971. Detective Chief Inspector Wyatt quickly tried to get a description of the two men, using the 'Photofit' technique, selected by Bob and amended by Beverley. These photofits were released to the papers for publication on 8th November, when it was also announced that a reward was being offered for information leading to an arrest and conviction.

Then came a break. They received an anonymous telephone call suggesting that one of the men involved was George Ince, a man with a criminal record, already under suspicion for a silver bullion heist carried out six months previously. The police suspected that the anonymous caller was less interested in the reward than in paying off a score against Ince, but it was true that his description did tally well with that of one of the robbers described by Bob and Beverley. Yet local enquiries brought into the frame two other men, unconnected with Ince – strangers who just twelve hours before the crime had asked a retired policeman the way to Rayne Road where the Barn stood. The ex-policeman gave a good description of the men, including the fact that one had a cast or some other deficiency in his right eye, while the other displayed a more outgoing and intelligent personality.

All the same, Ince was a prime suspect because of the tip-off and his previous record. Ince did have an alibi for the Barn job, one that he was reluctant to disclose because he had spent that night with his sweetheart Dolly, the wife of Charlie Kray, the most notorious, vicious gang leader in London's East End. But Ince *did* look like one of the photofit pictures, and when Beverley Patience, still in hospital but much improved, was shown a different photograph of Ince she almost excitedly confirmed 'That is the man!' At the time Bob did not see the likeness, although he changed his opinion as the case developed. The police intensified the search for Ince who, suspecting this, rang his home. Sister Phyllis confirmed what he had heard through the grapevine. The police were after him for the Barn murder – and they were armed. Ince rang his Dolly – she confirmed that he had stayed with her through the vital night and was ready to stand by him.

He hesitated for some days then, on 27th November, he took the tube to Theydon Bois where his solicitor was waiting in a car. Together they worked out a statement and then drove to Epping police station where George denied categorically any involvement at the Barn. Having given himself up he remained in custody far longer than ever he could have imagined, while the two robbers went free as the air. John Brook, when he read of the attention focussed on Ince, felt safe enough to resume his normal life and went on to get a job as a kitchen porter at the Salutation Hotel in Ambleside, moving from there to the Sutherland Restaurant in Bowness.

Ince was taken up to Braintree and the interviews and identity

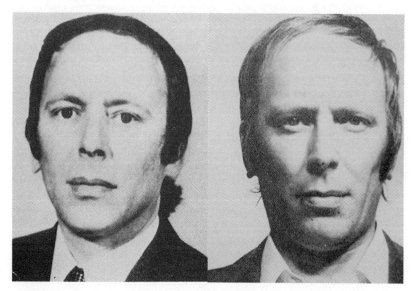

George Ince's passport photo, 1971.

George Ince after giving himself up in 1972.

parades began. Dolly Grey – she had changed her name by deed poll from Kray – had given George's solicitor a signed statement confirming his alibi, but that did not cut much ice. At 7.15 pm after an exhausting day of interviewing at Braintree Ince was taken off to Colchester and an identification parade in front of five witnesses who had been at the scene at the Barn the evening of the crime. The first one did not appear until 9.40 pm. She was Beverley Patience, and she touched him on the shoulder! Her father picked out another man; brother David 'thought' Ince was the man, and another person confidently identified him. That was enough on which to hold him, he was formally charged with the murder. By now it was midnight, George Ince had been kept on the go for over twelve hours, constantly protesting his innocence. Next morning he went before the Braintree magistrates and the police were allowed to keep him in custody while he underwent a second identity parade. Of eight witnesses only three identified him.

The police went on following up this false trail. A second man from the bullion robbery was traced, interviewed and eliminated, but the search went on down this avenue, though an analysis of the identifications made by the Patience family shows that their recall of the two men they saw that night was, understandably, unreliable. But the police were so convinced of George Ince's connection that they pressed on and were able to keep him in custody until 9th March 1973, when once more he was brought up before the Braintree magistrates and remanded to Brixton prison until he could be tried at the Chelmsford Crown Court in May. So Ince had already spent a long time in custody for a crime he had not committed, though he did have the matter of the bullion robbery still hanging over him.

In the interim the police tried to build up a case by checking round all his old associates. It led to wholesale raids of London's East End when all sorts of dirty linen was thoroughly washed – but that is another story. George Ince stood in the dock in the courtroom of the Shire Hall in Chelmsford on 2nd May 1973. He pleaded not guilty to murder, wounding and theft at the Barn. It was an unfortunate affair, with Ince clashing with an autocratic judge and then dismissing his counsel. The jury went out at about 3 pm and did not return until 9.30 pm when the foreman declared that they had been quite unable to agree a verdict. They were discharged and a new trial was ordered. Even for Ince who had already had a brush or two with the law, this was a harrowing experience.

On the following Monday a new trial began before a new judge. There were two interesting developments; the only forensic evidence against Ince was that two fibres of turquoise acrylic material on his overcoat exactly matched the material covering the lounge suite at the Barn, as analysed by Scotland Yard. Then it was revealed that George's sister Rose had a suite upholstered in exactly the same material but she had disposed of it to a neighbour some time after the police had collected George's coat. So now the identification relied only on the sight and recall of five witnesses. The second important factor was that Mrs Doris Grey, Ince's dear Dolly, came forward to support his wholly truthful alibi. With her husband Charlie Kray behind bars, but still a powerful influence outside, it was an extremely brave thing to do. The jury knew nothing of this mysterious lady other than that she and George were very much in love and had spent the night together. Because of the danger Dolly could be facing Ince was touchingly worried about her appearance in the witness-box. She was an excellent, emotive witness on his behalf. On 23rd May the jury was sent out to consider its verdict and after three hours came back with the verdict of 'Not guilty' on all charges. Family joy knew no bounds, but since George was still wanted for the bullion hijack he had to go back to Brixton to await yet another trial.

The police certainly had egg on their faces, but they were justified in pursuing the case by the positive identifications and the comments made at the trial by Beverley and her father. Where were they now to look for other suspects? Some of them, after all that work, could be forgiven for thinking that the right man was going free. Then as so often happens in life, they had a lucky break. It was the acorn which quickly grew into the oak tree.

Peter Hanson was nothing more than a small-time thief. He had done a break-in way up in Westmorland. Knowing the police were after him, he turned himself in, hoping thus to get a lighter sentence. His was a pretty relaxed interview. He told the story of all his movements, including a stay at the Salutation Hotel in Ambleside and the strange behaviour of a fellow he met there who bragged about his gun, his Beretta. He carried it round with him during the day, showed Hanson how it worked, even fired it out of a window one night. He slept with it concealed in his mattress, making a slit for that purpose, and even boasted openly during Ince's trial that Ince would not be found guilty because he, Brook, had shot the Patience family.

So, miles and miles from Essex, the police took up the threads of the case again. They followed Brook's movements from the hotel to the Sutherland Restaurant in Bowness, and there they arrested him on suspicion of being in possession of a firearm. While he was in the Kendal police station his flat in Windermere was thoroughly searched. The mattress was carefully examined. There was a slit, there was the Beretta, together with 14 rounds of ammunition. The Essex police were now brought in. The gun and the ammunition were checked against the bullets and cartridge cases found in the Barn attack. They matched! Now they had the murder weapon the police could forget George Ince and concentrate on this man Brook, but they still needed that second man.

They went about it very methodically. Friends? Brook seemed to have none. But he might have had criminal acquaintances, might have been 'banged up' at some time, perhaps sharing a cell with his accomplice. They checked the story of Brook's life through a number of prisons. Most telling, perhaps was that time he had been on the Pentonville parole scheme with a man who called himself Nicholas de Clare Johnson. They had worked together on a rehabilitation course. It was discovered that, with Brook released from prison on 13th October and Johnson allowed a weekend pass they could well have been together on the fateful night.

The evidence built up. A Mr Vane, Johnson's Romsey friend, entered in his diary that Johnson went to see him on the Sunday *after* the Barn job. An unfortunate coincidence meant that the police were unable to check this entry: when Johnson was finally released from prison in January 1973 he went to Romsey to spend a couple of weeks at Vane's house during which time poor Vane went to hospital for a minor operation, but did not survive it. That brief diary entry was the only evidence left of Johnson's previous visit. After Vane's death Johnson stayed for a bit in his friend's house before leaving in Vane's car, with the dead man's wallet. That is why he had been arrested and what he was being tried for on the very day in June when Essex police went to interview him at Southampton after he had spent a day in court. It was not long before he blurted out, 'Just charge me, I've had it on my mind for such a long time . . . I was expecting you . . . I was a coward to let another man stand trial.'

He had thought it would be a straightforward break-in and robbery at the Barn. He did not know Brook had a gun. If only, he said, Bob Patience had handed over that key straight away! No need to go over the details again. They were all put to the jury at the trial at Chelmsford Crown Court on Tuesday, 15th January 1974. Johnson stuck to his confession. Brook's counsel averred that his client lent Johnson the gun and that it was Ince who accompanied Johnson to the Barn. But Johnson's counsel talked of him being 'harnessed to a tiger' in the shape of Brook, and said that his act of compassion in fetching a towel for Mrs Patience's head wound showed a degree of compassion indicating that he was an unwilling partner in the shooting. Furthermore, he was actually out of the room when the last two shots were fired.

The end of the story came when the jury returned after four hours of deliberation. They found Brook guilty of murder and attempted murder and Johnson guilty of manslaughter. The former was sentenced by the judge to imprisonment for life on each of the three shootings while Johnson, a remorseful and unwilling partner in the dreadful crime, was sent to prison for ten years.

Index